December 24, 2021

Dear President Jimmy

I am writing to le
how much I LOVE you and
Mrs Rosalynn Carter and appreciate your
life's work that includes President/First lady
The Carter Center, Habitat For Humanity, for Prizes,
and above all as followers of Lord Jesus The Christ;
so far!!!

words ripped from a soul still bleeding

'LOVE, LIFE & PEACE'

poems for the future edition

the art of LOVE

Billy Lamont

billy lamont walk on water

~ the gift of my poetry ~
President Carter I had the pleasure to
meet you briefly in 1996 at your
book signing at The Book Revue in Huntington,
NY. At that time I gave you my first book
of poetry "the Gallery of Light" as a gift and
told you how much I enjoyed reading your
poetry, and could see Dylan Thomas inspiration
in it. I also shared that I was a follower of
Lord Jesus as you were signing my copy of
your wonderful book "Living Faith" that I enjoyed
immensely. So I thought perhaps You would enjoy
and be blessed by my latest book of poetry. I also
thought perhaps You would consider writing a cover
blurb for my future books of poetry if inspired.
Thank You for considering! YHWH, Jesus & the Holy Spirit Bless
You & your loved one,

~ sea with the eyes of angels!

#9781643456522

STRATTON
—PRESS—
Publishing Life

Words Ripped From A Soul Still Bleeding
Copyright © 2019 **Billy Lamont**

Stratton Press Publishing
831 N Tatnall Street Suite M #188,
Wilmington, DE 19801
www.stratton-press.com
1-888-323-7009

ISBN (Paperback): 978-1-64345-652-2
ISBN (Ebook): 978-1-64345-807-6

Printed in the United States of America

Acknowledgments

Cover Photograph: *Rory MacNish, rorymacnish.com*
Back Cover Photographs: *Mask Billy - Steven J. Messina; TV's On Stage - Rachel Lickter; Poet Priest King - Heather Ogiejko; Billy with Joe Strummer Street Art - Billy Lamont Self Portrait*
Cover Concept: *Billy Lamont*
Graphic Design: *Christopher "Circuit" Kelly*
Proofreading: *Lew Yedwab*

Thank you for your love, encouragement, support , and inspiration:
Keri Vannucci-Olson, Zion Lamont, William and Carmel Lamont, Robert, Barbara, Megan and Shawn Lamont, Kevin and Debbie Kavanaugh, the late Ned Kavanaugh and Rosemarie Kavanaugh, Bill and Karen Elefterion, the late Mary "Nana" Amoreno, Scott Boylan and Kim Olson-Boylan, Steven J. Messina, Lew Yedwab, Rory MacNish, Em Kruz, Steven A. Wolf, Dave Sharp, Scott Perry, Daniel and Sahani Fazzina, John and Anna Bembenek, Phil Accardi, Patti Smith, the late Jim Carroll, R.S. Pearson, Craig "Coconut" Santiago, Bethanne and Joseph Magazzo, Rob Carusso, Lily Elsayed, Jerry and Jackie Rooney, Doreen and Joanie Strathis, Rose Barnett, Michael Wolfgang Van, Kristie Malkasian, Bill Poulos, Bill Jarres, Andrew and Donna DeToll, the late monsignor Tom Hartman, Bobby Reidel, Pastor John Amandola Sr. and Saveria Amandola, Pastor John Amandola Jr. and Caryn Amandola, Danielle Campbell, Jon Soda James, Pastor Joshua and Rachel Lickter, Professor William J. Steedle, Cynthia Shor, Austin Smith, Colin Kasprowicz, Andrew Latham, Luke Haughwout, Seydina Senghor, Bob Dylan, Bono, The Edge, Larry Mullen Jr., Adam Clayton, Bob Holman, Shane Ries, Paula Curci, John Tabacco, Kevin Kovarik, the late Billy Capozzi and Finally Balanced, Ken Grimball, Slim Jim Phantom, Lisa "Kennedy" Montgomery, Rachel Perry, the late Joe Franklin, Khatia Shiuka, Noam Chomsky, the late Howard Zinn, and Ralph Nader. Paul Phillips, Jerry Thompson, Hershey Marquez, Jeff Reid, Vince Regis and everyone at Stratton Press.

Special thank you to: *Mike Peters and Jules Jones Peters of The Alarm, the late Allen Ginsberg, the late "Father Of Christian Rock" Larry Norman, Peter Garrett of Midnight Oil, the late Peace Activist/ Poet Daniel Berrigan, Steven Delopoulos of Burlap To Cashmere, Brian Ladd of Blackhouse, and Christopher "Circuit" Kelly.*

Contact Billy Lamont at The Other Perspective Management:
631-981-4780, TOPm777@gmail.com, billylamont.com
Facebook: facebook.com/poet.lamont;
Twitter: twitter.com/poetbillylamont;
Instagram: instagram.com/poetbillylamont; YouTube: sage777billy

TABLE OF CONTENTS

This book is dedicated to Father YHWH and Lord

JESUS, with THE HOLY SPIRIT bearing witness,

with deepest love and gratitude.

billy lamont

inspired by Dylan Thomas'
"Do Not Go Gentle Into That Good Night"
villanelle.
:)

Hero or Villain of My Villanelle?

You decide—Sheep or goat? Heaven or Hell?
Break down the fourth wall of art and culture!
Hero or villain of my villanelle?

Truth comes like ringing the Liberty Bell
Propaganda kills like a mad vulture
You decide—Sheep or goat? Heaven or Hell?

A turtle leaves the cover of his shell
A diamond forms under extreme pressure
Hero or villain of my villanelle?

Thirsty lips taste cool water from a well
Dignity offers hope, something more pure?
You decide—Sheep or goat? Heaven or Hell?

Poems bleed from my veins like ink from ink wells
Open wounds held to the light like torture
Hero or villain of my villanelle?

My words vibrate and create, can you tell?
Naked heart transparent without closure
You decide—Sheep or goat? Heaven or Hell?
Hero or villain of my villanelle?

1

dear reader

my friends are poets, writers,
philosophers, thinkers, prophets,
musicians and artists,
from throughout the ages,
that i read about in books

dear reader
perhaps in some simple way
i could be that for you

words are spoken from our intimate core
i can't suppress this passion and inspiration anymore

to be or not to be—
the art within the art within the art within the art
within the art
I want to feel—to have heart
to be real—to one day be the art!

brave enough to break down the healthy
or unhealthy boundary
that separates you from me
leaving only vulnerability
tearing down the fourth wall!
left only with the hope,
to one day, finally find
intimacy

i've broken the glass bubble of identity
reaching for your hand with sincerity
spiritual love is all inclusive

spiritual love knows no boundary
rather than alienation—i will always choose community!
stay connected/stay connected/stay connected
to be the change in the world
you and i want to see
i choose to live with integrity
to be the LOVE, be the LOVE, be the LOVE
to be the PEACE, to be the PEACE, to be the PEACE
i choose community over alienation!

soul metamorphosis
crucifixion
and resurrection
a poet that is a poem
a creation that can create
may your very soul be a great poem!!!
our life is a message
a string of pearls

society keeps telling me,
"you cannot write today
you have too many responsibilities"—
but when i do write
i will be ferocious!
when i write!
the page will bleed
and be blessed with insight
when i write
when i write!

I BELIEVE DREAM PEACE poem:
The Scriptures recording

The poem I BELIEVE DREAM PEACE *is for my beloved longtime friend Mike Peters of The Alarm's* The Scripture's *recording to benefit Love Hope Strength Foundation and those fighting cancer internationally. It was written to help foster peace in the Holy Land of the Middle East, by helping find bone marrow matches for Muslims, Christians, and Jews fighting cancer there.*

I was awarded a Guinness World Record for my contribution to the The Scriptures *recording, which is the "Longest Officially Released Song Ever."*

Parts of I BELIEVE DREAM PEACE *were written at John Lennon's Childhood Home at a "Protest Of All Future Wars Before They Even Begin" event and The Cavern Club in Liverpool, England, in January 2014 prior to my knowledge that I would be participating in this wonderful, epic recording. I recited this poem in one take as Mike Peters recorded me backstage before a show he was doing at the Iridium Jazz Club, on Broadway, in New York City. Interestingly the final musician contributions, mix down and mastering were completed later that year at The Beatles legendary Abbey Road Studios in London, England.*

[poet billy lamont]

I BELIEVE DREAM PEACE

Muslim, Christian, and Jew
it was written in the scriptures of life
LOVE is written in the scriptures of life

I. a table

the way you're tearing at me
and i'm pushing at you
not a healthy friction
like dancing without any rhythm
being swift to speak
and then slow to listen

i never wanted more than my portion
i wish i could sit at your table
but all the chairs are broken
we used to eat off the same plate
but now we cannot even coexist
in the same room
i desire to see your face shine with life
and leave this place of sleepy gloom

who are we underneath our skin?
does anyone love anyone?
are we as good as we say we are?

the way we silently stare
it's like we have given up
on trying to communicate
when there isn't any understanding
it's like being alone
trying to carry a really heavy weight

i've learned you can't fix an emotion
but you can rebuild trust
when it has been broken
the way we're unequally yoked together
it's like a dove is trying to fly
attached to an anchor

where's the love when we constantly fight?
just because we argue like lawyers
don't make us right

who are we underneath our skin?
does anyone love anyone?
are we as good as we say we are?

II. hypocrisy 666

hy.poc.ri/sy dance/s
to the scrip/tur/al twist
o/pen hand, a closed fist

III. spiritual orphans

spiritual orphans better have the skill
to persuade everyone at church
that they are true
when love is not enough
wish i was perfectly holy like you

[an artist is not less of a person
time to claim my place in all of creation]

i can't make you love me
love is a choice, a choice
you're not thinking of me
i'm choking on these words, losing my voice
you're not standing above me
life should sing out with joy and rejoice
i can't make you love me
love is a choice

meeting your needs
like serving a cruel task master
demanding more than i could possibly give
and faster, faster

[your perception is a distortion of holy creation]

hearts and minds, hearts and minds
[life should be a work of art]
hearts and minds, hearts and minds
[use you strong mind, loving heart]
~LOVE, intelligence of the heart will light your mind~

i can't make you love me
love is a choice, a choice

IV. i believe dream peace

Muslim, Christian, and Jew
it was written in the scriptures of life
LOVE is written in the scriptures of life

the holy land, peace, and I
are bound together by fate
LOVE will always conquer hate

propaganda tongue has gone to war
language hijacked, kidnapped
and held hostage

[religion fueled hatred—the worst kind of hate
violence and death is her soulmate]

propaganda mind brainwashes
and murders through soulless uniform
conform to the norm
and another precious wife will lose her husband lover
 another daughter without her beloved father
another mother will lose her treasured son
we stand in protest of all future wars
before they have even begun!

[redemption, transformation of holy creation]

like reading poetry
with empathy—
wisdom from different cultures

and subcultures
throughout the centuries
let's gain an understanding
and really listen to each other
with tolerance and compassion
and like my lover lays her head on my shoulder
and walks beside me
let's walk together in community

Khatia and I
having coffee with the philosopher Diogenes
we are looking for a REAL HUMAN!
beautiful darling Khatia
is a poem without words
like Nico of the Velvet Underground
she is my mirror
I am poema—the poem
a poet that is a poem—my life is a message
I am DADA*
DA DA DA DA DA
and DADA IS EVERYWHERE!!!
She is rock and roll freedom
Albert Einstein tells soldiers, "JUST SAY NO!"
John Lennon, Charlie Chaplin, Patti Smith, Khatia and I
dance at the Van Gogh-a-go-go
GO! GO!!
Martin Luther King, Mahatma Gandhi, Daniel Berrigan,
JESUS The Christ,
Jules and Mike Peters
dance at the Van Gogh-a-go-go
GO! GO!!

YOU too, U2 and Bono
GO! GO!!
A REAL HUMAN is not a uniform!
You are I and I you
LOVE

you are
I and I
you
LOVE
I BELIEVE DREAM PEACE

it was written in the scriptures of LIFE
PEACE was written in the scriptures of GOD
LOVE, LOVE was written in the scriptures of LIFE
HOPE, HOPE was written in the scriptures of LIFE
STRENGTH, STRENGTH was written in the scriptures of
LIFE

LOVE, HOPE, STRENGTH
LOVE HOPE STRENGTH
I BELIEVE DREAM PEACE

Note: Dadaism is an avant-garde art movement that began in the early 20th century.

HELL NO MONSANTO!
(Label Your GMO—Genetically Modified Orgasm)

frickin' frackin'
corporate weenie whackin'
listen to my rant yo—
HELL NO MONSANTO!
label your GMO!
your poison seed is a disease!
a genetically engineered weed
mutated, just like your patent on greed
a contaminated seed that just won't grow
HELL NO MONSANTO!

senator puppet corporate troll
innocent blood population control

the world is global warming
the middle class is slowly deforming
the masses are enslaved and conforming

Monsanto, let's hear your statement yo—
for marketing your contamination and death product
while branding our woe
for not labeling your GMO!
Genetically Modified Orgasm

lips pursed together tightly
no comment guilty
it's just like you were born yesterday
while secretly buying out our food supply
with your filthy money
making the world safe for the greedy
you're a suit without a soul, a troll

trying to sell us illuminati population control

media censor has me on mute
as they sell the masses a news story that is cute

the criminal elite drilling for oil
and then shooting their rusty load
coming, coming out of our families' kitchen faucets
frickin' frackin'
corporate weenie whackin'

Monsanto, hell no yo—
your poison seed is a disease
and won't grow!
it's even in Gerber baby food
and We The People are now in the know
HELL NO MONSANTO!
let's ban your GMO! let's ban your GMO!

engineering our food with genetics
is like outlawing health and organics

propaganda mind poison food
greedy guilty vomiting
propaganda mind poison food
senator puppet corporate troll
innocent blood population control!
HELL NO MONSANTO!

*Written in March 2014 and was recited to kick off March Against
Monsanto protest at Union Square, New York City and Worldwide.*

i-uh-wanna-pee-ah! onomatopoeia

Oh no!
i drank way too much water
before this loooooooong   car ride
i-uh-wanna-pee-ahhh!
onomatopoeia

oxyMORON

as anyone who knows me will attest
i am—

an everyday extraordinary
earthy spiritual
a normal eccentric
an average oddity
a standard quirky
that is irrelevantly relevant
and ordinarily complex

like an imperfectly perfect diamond
that has attained an imbalanced balance
to be dysfunctionally compatible with others,
i guess you could call me
a beautiful mess

simply A HUGE
oxyMORON
am i

Lucy-Fur

i'm on the devil's hit list
but Lucy-Fur
the height of soulless tyranny
will never allure
or distract me
detract and subtract me
deceive, mislead, entrap, and attack me
Lucy-Fur will never be
able to whack me
stigmatize and subtract me
i am saving souls for eternity
by the passion and blood of Lord JESUS
and the word of my testimony!

her curves, my angles

Although your mouth was sweet and spoke of triviality
Your eyes were sincere and mirrored reality

Her rhythm pulsates and vibrates
like an inviting river flowing
My motion is firm and hard and steady
like the mighty ship I am rowing

her curves ~~
my angles ^>
her curves ~~
my angles ^>

Her form is where grace and beauty flows
like a ballerina spinning on her toes

My soft, gentle touch awakens skin
like it can only be when real love caresses from within
I flirt, you tease
souls touch

her curves ~~
my angles ^>
her curves ~~
my angles ^>

My heart is sensitive and my strong body flows
like the meter in this poet's prose

She opens to pure love like a wildflower in the sun
Oh, the beautiful way she sways and slides
On the downbeat, my strong pointed thrust collides
My love is like explosions of fireworks on the inside,
my bride

Our dance, she comes close and then moves away
Her lovely motion like a ballet
My dance more rough around the edges, you can get cut
If you rub against me the wrong way

her curves ~~
my angles ^>
her curves ~~
my angles ^>

Her coloratura soprano is the passion in opera
Her love is like her sweet breaths and comes in deep sighs
I sing in the warm silences—
the melody of love deep within my eyes

her curves ~~
my angles ^>
her curves ~~
my angles ^>

Her form is where grace and beauty flows
ike a ballerina spinning,
spinning on her toes

mtv

everyone says that with mtv in the 80s,
"video killed the radio star"
but i say that with mtv in the 90s
"reality shows killed the tv star"

Theater of Roses

the spotlight is too bright tonight
people think I'm acting when I'm on stage
but the pain is real!
can the audience hear me?

how come I am so lonely in such a crowded room?
social solitaire in a theater of roses

I must concentrate on my performance
my mind is wandering

I have to perform
With everyone's eyes on me
Need everyone's applause
To be what I want to be
Am I confident and secure?
Or is it just another flaw
In my personality

someone once told me I was self-centered
I know I am not
I do not have enough self-esteem
maybe I am self-absorbed but not selfish
there is a difference

words can be like switchblades

I was born to create
a creation that creates
   - a curse -

I am better at performing than living life
am i like Charles Baudelaire's albatross?
   "whose giant wings hinder him from walking"
am i too sensitive to live?

when I am confused and vulnerable
I am easy prey
prey/pray prey/pray
the apostle Paul said in the Bible—
   "cast off the works of darkness and put on the
   armor of light"
can life be spiritual?

as an adult I still play like children do
I make art
my imagination never dies
it just gets stronger and stronger

I was born to create
a creation that creates
   -a gift-

Albert Einstein said—
   "imagination is better than knowledge"
I like that
I have always created a niche in which to live
created my own world
sometimes this scares me
I am afraid I will not find my way back into the real world—
maybe that's okay—reality is not always your friend—

I am like Franz Kafka's hunger artist—
  "who fasts because he cannot find
  the food he likes"
is that strange?
or am I just living life artistically?

life is spiritual
  -balance-
my life was created
I create my life

life is spiritual
but most people are asleep

Plato said in The Cave—
  "the bewilderment of the eyes are of two kinds
  and arise from two causes, either from coming
  out of the light or from going into the light"

the audience—
eyes that are black
eyes that are rainbows
eyes that are daggers
eyes that are roses
eyes that are graveyards
eyes that are candles

look into my eyes—
look into my soul!

I am an enigma to be gazed upon
analyzed
psychoanalyzed
always to be applauded
but never to be loved

LOVE is a revolution

the revolution
is spiritual evolution
battling the forces of entropy
the opposite of love is not hate
it is apathy
& LOVE,
LOVE is a revolution!!!

u.s./us rights left?

there is no left   there is no right
democrats   and republicans
                        are in the same club
there is no left   there is no right
                        just the top
                        and the bottom
                        the rich
                        and the peasants
                        the haves
                        and the have-nots

            the few percent of this world's people that are rich
                    own and control almost everything!

                                            the church is in bed
                                            with conservatives
                                            the right tells the church
                                            to not care about the environment
                                            this could hurt corporate
                                            false prophets
                                            oops i mean profits

on the left
being perceived as
caring about the environment
is a good way to get elected

                                            pastors as CEOs
                                            christian right?
                                            christian white

democrats are no longer left
no one left left

liberty
you are free   you are free to consume
purchase your own slice of gloom
                              why should we stop shopping?
bombs are dropping!

            when a few companies
            own everything

                              freedom of speech
is so far out of reach
            at what point should we resist?

                              too busy trying to survive
to be alive
                              greed is restructuring

            taking our jobs
            grabbing our pay
now you have the nerve   to steal
                              our retirement 401k

medical care by   insurance companies
                              not by doctors

      we keep hearing about the war on terror
            but what about the war on labor?

                              campaign for u.s.
campaign for us
                              oil for u.s.

in the interest of us   us?

                    i love america

                              but are american interests

                    our interests?

                              or nationalism disguised
as patriotism

                              welfare for the rich
tax breaks for the rich
                              through brute force
and torture
                              colonization then and now

there is no left   there is no right

                    only issues in stereo
                    invent
                    think for yourself
                    fulfill your potential
                    there are higher possibilities

                              judicial tyranny
still need healthy boundaries

                    checks and balances
                    what are the house
                    and senate afraid of?

judicial tyranny

don't they need
search warrants
to search your house?

monitoring innocent people

guilty till proven innocent?
we the people
are not terrorists
we have rights
not just the right to remain silent
not just the right to pay taxes
at what point should we resist?

still need healthy boundaries
towards the left
pro choice
have a voice
pro choice
please choose life not death left!

judicial tyranny
corporate criminals

our rights

have left?

our rights   our rights

have left!

money will trickle down

pay your taxes

the only thing that trickles down
is piss droplets
from the criminal elite's penis,   right?
shake it off
shake it off
the people's trust

executive criminal
criminal elite
retreat
here comes the street!

class of thieves
THE HOLY SPIRIT grieves
capitalism's got a black eye
more than the usual greedy stye

soundbite thought pattern
we will uncover the truth beneath
awaken the wisdom in the chaos
the underlying love, silence, peace in the noise

renegades of hope
outlaws of love
join the resistance
before it's too late!

what's happening?
better call the green party
someone telephone ralph nader
can't blame michael moore
better ask noam chomsky!

This poem was written in 2004. My favorite recital of this poem was at Occupy Wall Street, NY City on October 5, 2011.

transcend 777

life like art that bleeds pure soul
transcend the trend, dare to feel
to have heart, to be for real!

life as a poet: hooked on phonics anonymous

i feel like a jerk
my personality has a quirk
& i hate to network

but you—you are a living action verb
your syntax is superb
can i please have a cover blurb?
***** ***** ***** ***** ***** *****

i'm sorry i tried
wish i could make you a bride
it's just that i am more committed to
living vicariously through poets who have died

i cling to you because i'm in a deep depression
you are a beautiful obsession
but i—i am not your possession!
***** ***** ***** ***** ***** *****

i can't pay my bills
lost all my social skills
but i have a new poem that kills

my boss won't give me a raise
but i can really turn a phrase
please give me your praise!
***** ***** ***** ***** ***** *****

i am easily pissed
an extraordinarily temperamental artist
do you want to be on my guest list?

i live with too much conviction
have to work on my diction
& my bio is fiction
in short, i'm addicted to addiction!
***** ***** ***** ***** ***** *****

     poetry & suffering
     were sometimes synonymous
     until i joined "hooked on phonics anonymous"

Attention: Wannabeats

attention: wannabeats
yeah, all who are entering the world of the spoken word

my agent tells me:
   "you have a gift
   it's okay to be weird
   just as long as you have
   a goatee or a beard
   poetry is a trend
   & i am your friend
   so buy a beret
   & pretend that you're gay
   & put on your best james dean face
   or strike a gangster pose
   & we'll market your fears and woes
   all you have to do is—
   pick my nose
   lick my toes
   & never, ever wash your clothes
   & you'll be doing sold out shows!"

well, mr. suit-and-tie has perfect hair
& i never trust anyone with perfect hair
& he keeps smiling at me
& shaking my hand
he tells me to leave my message
at the sound of his tone
i would, but i'm tone-deaf
& the starving artist feeds my soul
the starving artist feeds my soul!

whatever happened to sitting in a cafe
& discussing poetry?
instead you tell me of career opportunities—
poets are in television shows, radio commercials
& movies
you tell me you are going to leave your mark
well, you already have & just don't know it
it's just too bad it's a skid-mark
on your underwear!

all my friends know i curse
greeting card verse
& everyone knows
i dream in prose
anyone can write down words on paper
but not everyone has soul!

in the eighties tough guys wanted to beat me
with baseball bats
because i was a poet
well, actually this happened once in the nineties too
i guess this is the closest I have ever been
to really being a beat poet!

in the eighties everyone thought
i was eccentric
& told me i was just a freak
well, don't feel too bad for me
no need to tweak
because now it's the 21st century
& geek is chic this week!

& i am just a freak
a freak who is no longer a writer:
i email letters
do interviews
do lunch
send out press releases
& return phone calls

poetry as a trend
blows my brain
& now i'm insane
but that's okay
because when you're crazy
everything you write is poetry!

one thing you will learn hanging out with me
is that poets
in the 21st century
need secretaries!

528 poems

the fabric of love's
heart tone
YHWH vibrates at 528

the color of sound
a breath
YHWH vibrates at 528

universal code
JESUS
mathematical matrix of love

the tonality
of love
Keri vibrates at 528

her vocalized breath
pure love
Keri vibrates at 528

the fragrance of light
soulmate
Keri vibrates at 528

my heart resonates
pure love
Keri vibrates at 528

my home and soulmate
pure love
Keri vibrates at 528

the flavor of fire
her love
Keri vibrates at 528

Pure love resonates
soulmate
Keri vibrates at 528

Dedicated to my fiancée, Keri Vannucci-Olson

7 reflections for jim carroll

1. inspiration

in a sweaty upstairs apartment
of a small cape cod house in east northport, long island
on scorching hot 90-degree summer days in 1989
two young men feverishly play vinyl records
and pray for their inspirations—
u2, the alarm, the beatles, patti smith, the doors,
skinny puppy and the jim carroll band
a young poet screams his lyrics into a microphone and
a sound effects module until he no longer has a voice,
or is he finding his voice?
the toxic banana's guitar is cranked up
distortion and effects pedals color the notes blazing
through the humidity
on fire with the passion of a new dream, to give hope
happy nightmare!

2. a poet

when you first start out
no one tells you about the loneliness
essential to being a poet
perhaps it is buried in the pages of an old baudelaire book
the poem the albatross
that a sexy young lover once gave me
few tell you the price of such illumination
of living so passionately and without boundaries
like you jim
"the cost of such height and vision
while secretly wishing you were down in the stadium
with others"

the cost of being driven to write so tirelessly through
the night
to form the perfect couplet
skillfully chiseling the words of a new poem
from left over postmodern iron and steel
without the luxury of marble in this robot naked culture
no one chooses to be a writer
a writer has to write
and if he is not allowed to; he will write even more
ferociously and desperately

imagination with expression
and heart
the blessing and a curse

jim, you did it all
on the alleyway sufferings, you shined a light
and then shouted it off new york city rooftops
in the middle of the night
and kept us laughing with your backstreets humor
all the while

jim, i'm remembering you today
a new york poet, diarist, musician—a brilliant artist
an early inspiration that would metamorphose
into an acquaintance/friend
i'm remembering you today
as i sit and drink this strong cup of coffee
in this lonely existential cafe
on a freezing february afternoon in 2010
i will always remember you...
and I SALUTE YOU, BROTHER!!!!!!!

jim, you never were some warhol art experiment
more than some cruel and demented
sociological study of misfits and artists
given drugs and then filmed to see who is the strongest
like some first sick reality tv show, the real *piss factory*
you were much more than that! (you smiled and agreed
when i said this to you)
(note: i'm not talking about lou reed and
the velvet underground they are fabulous!)
you have a rare artist soul
overlooked, used, misunderstood, and tortured
you were new york city's own arthur rimbaud!

jim, in your later years
i believe my prayers wrapped around you
like God's grace
like the prayer cloth you told me you wore
when you were younger
after keith richards gave it to you

like your mother's fervent prayers for you
during your teenage years
still echo through eternity
and found God's hearing ears
Jesus didn't hurt you the way the church did
Jesus stood beside you
Jesus shed bloody heart tears for you

bloody—

like the words ripped from your soul
still bloody
as you sculpted the poem
that wanted to be born
or exorcised from your spirit

remembering
a remarkable new york poet
and the power of the avant-garde
you were not interested in titles or degrees
just raw poems ripped from real souls, still bloody
raw like scrapes after hitting the pavement
of a city downtown street on a scorching summer day
after you just made a game winning lay up
in a basketball game with such form, style, and grace
before the fall

3. death: memorandum

jim,
you died at your desk
writing
doing what you love
 joyful

~your heart fainted before your new masterpiece
the petting zoo
before the glory that passed through you
and graced the page~

4. the wake: synchronicity

a single long-stemmed red rose on a closed coffin
i arrived after most of the others
i think i may have been the only one
who kneeled and prayed
by your coffin
patti smith said you are now with her other friends
who passed on
robert mapplethorpe, allen ginsberg, william burroughs
her beloved fred "sonic" smith

at the appropriate time
compassion and love brought me to the front of the room
to speak
it was like i was in slow motion with the room filled with
your catholic family, friends, and ny punk legends
all out of focus listening
it was like i was called to be the perfect odd fit
for this moment
as i awkwardly and nervously
shared the heartfelt gift of blessed hope given to me

jim, here's synchronicity for you:
[like your *8 fragments for kurt cobain*]
it was like i already had a memorial service for you
when my best friend
called with the news about you on a monday—
said you broke on through to the other side on friday—
that sunday afternoon i had encouraged my neighbor
she had been minutes from death on saturday night

i told her of the prayers i said for her that night
how the ambulance crew fought to keep her alive
how they resuscitated her
7 feet from where i sleep
while my son enjoyed the gift of sleep without ever waking
i told her how happy i was that she was still alive
and i spoke of you, jim
your life and art
i needed an example of life's wonder and a reason
for her to live
and the only words i could think of were yours,
"you could have gone to florence
and looked into the eyes of bellini or raphael's portraits"

jim, did you stop by to say goodbye to me
on the way home to eternity?
or did an angel bring you to mind
to help a sister in distress?
it felt like you were there alive
as alive as my son choosing to play on the wood floor
that my neighbor laid upon twelve hours before
moments from death
as alive as this woman still was
it was like i already had a memorial service for you
i don't know what it means
but felt driven to share it with your family of friends
at the wake
felt driven to share that news that
you were alive in eternity,
"like it was news delivered
from a distant galaxy"

you are still alive in eternity
just in a different form
you live on in your poetry
and we will see you again!

jim, you were no saint
but you are a saint
when you believe in Jesus
when you secretly light a candle for a friend—
the apostle paul called his congregation
"saints" in his letters
the greek word means "holy ones"
it's not about you
or them—the church
or me
in the end anyway
i will let you down
i will let you down
it's all about The One
God, YAHWEH!
and His awesome grace!!!!!!!!

i found myself stumbling out of the wake
on to cobblestone streets of the west village
and little italy
until the friendship of the jim carroll band
surrounded me and invited me to a cafe—
dinner with terrell and steven
and their loved ones
glad i had the company of some artists
that night

and such great ones!
i told them of early inspiration,
"the city drops into the night,"
"it ain't hip to sink that low unless you plan a resurrection"
good conversation
warm southern fried chicken
laughs
and a bottle of red wine

5. the funeral: mystical

the next morning i walked down carmine street
where my beloved nana lived in the 1920s and 30s
until she moved to long island
carmine street is where our lady of pompei
catholic church is
where jim's funeral was
inside the church a women sang the most beautiful
ave maria i have ever heard
it resonated and echoed up to Heaven
with pure passion
it felt like my beloved nana
was sitting next to me
and holding my hand in church
like when i was a child
ave maria was her favorite song
she passed on when i was a teenager
thought it broke my heart forever
but felt her undying love vibrating in my sacred heart
that day
~a realization~

this is an old catholic church in my nana's old neighborhood
my nana must have gone to this church
i later found out this was her home church
and that she married my grandfather in that church
in the 1930s

the mass
and holy communion
i overheard one man say he hadn't had communion
in 30 years
until that day

my prayers for you, jim
were given *wings*
transformed into song by patti smith
her heart's passion coalesced with mine
in one voice
one spirit

outside the church
patti, i wanted to hold you
to comfort you
kiss away all your beautiful pure tears
pure like your heart rhythms
pure like your natural beauty
you were kind and generous
when you said that you were glad i spoke at the wake
your mystical heart somehow understood
for a moment i didn't feel lonely
i couldn't even answer you
just stuttered, stared, and touched my heart
it was beyond words anyway

6. meditations and reflections on the funeral

the funeral, the funeral
don't want to be oversensitive
or hyper-spiritual
it's more natural for me to be cynical

the funeral, the funeral
don't want to be oversensitive
or hyper-spiritual
but it was kind of mystical
it felt like i was looking through a crystal
with light being purified and filtered by God
before it fragments and shines out in different colors
crimson red like Jesus's blood
like italian red wine
purple like luther's
"royal priesthood of the everyday believer"
majestic like love from the common man

the funeral, the funeral
don't want to be oversensitive
or hyper-spiritual
maybe it's even more mystical
more like God's pure light shining through me
in this poem
like sunlight passing through the stained glass window
of an ancient catholic church
God shining through the different colors
of an artist's personality
rare gem-like colors
on the church floor

covering the dirt that
no one sees

the funeral, the funeral
i decided to leave before the burial

***

the paradox
Jesus was 100% man
100% God
the paradox
we are 100% men and women
but when we believe in Jesus
we receive forgiveness and the promise of eternity
we receive The Holy Spirit
we have God 100% in us
and everything becomes pure

7. pure

jim,
pure...
pure the way you liked your heroin when you were a street kid
pure like your mother's prayers in your teenage years
pure like ointment on an old church wound
pure like the raw power of your writing and art
pure like the integrity of a punk song
pure like your inspiration and our new year's day conversations
pure like my nana's prayers for me through the night
when i went out to party as a teenager
pure like my nana's love when i didn't deserve it
pure like *ave maria* sung in an old church in little Italy

pure like patti's tears and song of mourning for you
pure like fire
and then beauty risen from the ashes
pure like forgiveness and dinner with new friends
pure like a kind and loving heart

pure like white
white untouched freshly fallen snow
on new york city streets
pure like your white shroud
Jesus's burial cloth
the shroud of turin

pure
like grace

*Written for my friend Jim Carroll, NY poet and author of The Basketball
Diaries, shortly after his passing on into eternity. September 11, 2009–
February 9, 2010*

BEYOND BABYLON: A Word of Explanation

The title of my latest album Beyond Babylon *was suggested by a close friend, singer/songwriter Steven A. Wolf. I recorded 90% of its poetry in a single take, in one hour, in a recording studio on September 19th, 2012, with the thought that it would be a gift for my son, Zion Lamont. The inspiration that moved me was the previous years of being a single father to Zion (well sort of with joint custody) and living in my hometown of Babylon, NY. This inspiration also centered around Psalm 137 in the Holy Bible, "By the waters of Babylon I wept for Zion." I even did a video blog explaining this at the Babylon Village Dock and published it to YouTube.com a few days later. In essence, this poetry is words of hope within the disorientation of personal suffering and brokenness.*

Hurricane Sandy devastated my hometown and surrounding areas on October 29th, 2012. Like many of my neighbors, I soon began giving practical help to local victims. Aid organizations, church leaders, and various neighbors recognized me as the poet who has appeared on national television and done book signings at major bookstores in local malls.

I was invited to recite my poetry at numerous outreach events for hurricane victims. My heart was very grieved and filled with sadness for the Hurricane Sandy victims, and I had a lot of new poetry that I had recorded but not released as an album (until October 2013) that felt as if it was written for this situation, so I began reciting it. The poetry, the local town references and symbols in Beyond Babylon, *took on a greater meaning for others as I shared it.*

I performed the entire Beyond Babylon *album as a multimedia show with performance art and electronic and Americana pop music and synchronized film projected at Historic Babylon Town Hall when the CD/digital download was released by major distributors internationally in October 2013. FEMA (Federal Emergency Management Agency) was present at my request to offer practical counseling to any of the town of Babylon residents that were in attendance and may be suffering storm-related trauma.*

It is powerful the healing within this poetry and music, something greater than I, so I am very grateful to have been a part of this sacred art and trying to just stay out of the way of it. I hope the Beyond Babylon *section of this book can touch and inspire you to* Imagine A Day!!!

[poet billy lamont]

like marconi...(SOS—save our soul—prologue)

like marconi...
like marconi sending the first wireless message to sea
heart transmissions bouncing off of holy satellite
my prayers blessed vibrations traveling into eternity
and the stars look so different tonight

"by the waters of Babylon
i wept for Zion"
~Psalms, The Holy Bible~

words go on and on
resonating through time and space
eternity
like memory...

scattered (dizzy)

fighting unclear
out-of-focus mind is scattered
as this new york city heart
has been shattered

how do I get my heart beating again?
where has all my passion gone?
it takes all my energy just trying to survive
it's time to be alive!

i'm feeling dizzy
i need to sit down
sacred heart is beating
but i can't hear the sound
i'm dizzy
dizzy
everything is spinning around

need time to think
process all this information overload
not sleeping for days like slow torture
i will never implode!

what's worse greed or fear?
feeling the heaviness that gives birth
to compassion right here

i'm feeling dizzy
i need to slow down
sacred heart is beating
but i can't hear the sound

i'm dizzy
dizzy
everything is spinning around

soundbite thought pattern
we will uncover the truth beneath
awaken the wisdom in the chaos
find the underlying love, silence and peace in the noise

my arms are bruised
but will never tire
of upholding life

all life was formed
has become deformed
needs to be reformed
all life and creation can be redeemed!

i'm feeling dizzy
i need to sit down
sacred heart is beating, beating
but i can't hear the sound
i'm dizzy
dizzy
everything is spinning around

love, when will this fever finally break?
love, touch me and soothe this heartache
love, give love
love, give love

God is as close as your breath
as close as every beat of your heart

can you see the wisdom
my blood on these pages?
my poems are like fragments of light
tiny pieces of my soul on paper

argyle park

I.
i woke up
i woke up dreaming
i woke up
i woke up
i woke up screaming
lying on a park bench—
lightning is stabbing the dark canvas of the night sky
i had been out walking
under a full moon
a pure heart cries out for LIFE
with PASSION as bright as the stars—
now my muddy boots
fight to stand up in this sinking sand

i will show you my nakedness
open wounds and the scars
i too have suffered
and found refuge
in argyle park

II.
i remember
i remember first love
heart poems
written on blank pages of new books
exchanged by candlelight
and later returned in tears
first love
a tear droplet and a promise

first love
severed
first love
left one
torn in two

when i was nineteen years old
suffered my first broken heart
by the concrete waterfalls
of argyle park

III.
in a dark corner of the park
albert einstein walked up to me
and whispered,
"it's become appallingly clear that our technology
has surpassed our humanity"
in the distance a train pulls out of the babylon station
commuters leave home and family to go to work
blindfolded walkers never see light
corporations and the materialistic
treat people like they are interchangeable
like they are disposable
disposable
disposable people
brainwashed by the media and all those commercials
hypnotized into mindless clones
men and women only trying to live their lives
to provide food and shelter for their families
not just die with the whimper of a drone
blindfolded walkers never see light

IV.
if you believe the lie
i will not attend the funeral for your heart and mind
you are not their product!
and I am not for sale!
the scars are now visible
the wrinkles around my eyes are beginning to show
my brokenness now spoken—
PASSION burns the page
of a simple notebook
this poem is alive!
ALIVE!
rip it out
set it on fire!
It's alive in the sacred heart
I am ALIVE!
breathing, feeling, sensing, loving, holy awake
asking, searching, pleading, begging, bleeding,
scratching the darkness of the night sky for something real!

when we were younger
klayton took a long look into the poet's eye
later lvl, buka, and klank shrieked out
under the same ruthless stars

the sensitive artist soul has been tortured
been falsely accused and mocked
for a season fell a victim—
the sky is darker than dark
tonight I find sanctum
in argyle park

i woke up
i woke up dreaming
i woke up
i woke up
i woke up screaming
laying on a park bench—
the stars, tiny pinholes of light shining through the night sky
memories swirl like lifetimes
I had been out walking
after dark
this moment still screams with PASSION
on fire alone in argyle park

For Klayton, Lvl, Buka and Klank

pure white light

the persistence
the persistence of memory
like the painting by salvador dali
my darling, dance with me on the edge of night!
dance with me until new love sings with first light!

a pure heart is keenly vulnerable
when a heart fully charged with love is rejected
the soul's wound is horrible!
in this solitary moment Lord i pray
baptize my naked soul with grace in motion
real LOVE is greater than a feeling or emotion
the cross precedes the crown but for a season!

shhh...the language of this mystic dawn
is yet to be born in the words of the poet priest king
visionary dreamer
sense the intuitive abstract spiritual
time is infinite
& time is finite
& this suffering is only for a season!
pure white light
my darling, dance with me on the edge of night!
dance with me until new love sings with first light!

pure white light
tranquil center
enter LOVE

white, the harmony from which all color was created
white, the harmony from which all color was created

blessed hope beyond babylon

*Inspired by singer/songwriter Steven Delopoulos of Burlap To
Cashmere's music*

haiku-a-cuckoos

sister on the street
looking for love,not a screw
haiku-a-cuckoo

work and slave all day
family times are too few
haiku-a-cuckoo

look at me cross-eyed
or unkindly and i'll sue
haiku-a-cuckoo

do not tell the truth
hide it whatever you do
haiku-a-cuckoo

i talk to myself
and never listen to you
haiku-a-cuckoo

Dedicated to Brian Ladd of Blackhouse

self interview/self portrait [a postmodern dada]

self interview—
the problem of suffering
<—pascal talk some sense into me
—>franz kafka is stalking me
—>baudelaire mind is thinking me
<—need to wash my mind with The Holy Bible
<—and then dry it with r. s. pearson philosophy

I woke up dreaming of Christian reformation
senses reeling with andré breton's surrealism manifesto
went drinking with martin luther and bono
discussed theology in the corner pub
pints of ale and irish whiskey
clashing with The Holy Bible in my soul
like holy rock and roll—
we shared belly laughs
and prayers for the common man

I stepped outside into the cool fall air
alone
lit a miniature cigar from santo domingo
and took a slow drag
soul of sky was masked by a nuclear cloud
did someone cut me?
   didn't realize I was slowly bleeding
did you warn me?
   sorry I wasn't listening

~stoic survival~

like a wound with a new stitch
like a nervous twitch
I've been living on the border of an unfulfilled wish
the local town's church bell rings out
faithfully, as it always does
every hour
The Spirit is the same
but the times sure have changed

mirror perspective
a photograph
I am an outsider amongst outsiders
a rebel amongst rebels
never could find the outside of society for me
in this subculture of conformity
<—The Holy Bible is the message guiding me
<—kierkegaard's writing like a lamp illuminating me
<—escher's lines keep redefining me
<—Lord have mercy

self portrait—   ^

GOD is...   I am...

GOD is...   I am...

GOD is my dada   JESUS is the wonderful I AM

I think you like picasso, all perspectives at once
[bet this is how GOD sees it]

feel you passionately like van gogh
[i know this is GOD's holy passion]

love and kiss her like klimt's "the kiss"
[know GOD's desire for us through this]

i see JESUS THE CHRIST's cross like dali
[awakens me to GOD's higher view; JESUS's amazing
power, infinite love and humility]

have i expressed this like jackson pollack's paint drippings?
[oh, to be a unique splash of color in God's expressionistic
masterpiece!]

I AM
I AM
JESUS IS the magnificent I AM!

For R. S. Pearson

a van gogh morning

well, it's a van gogh morning on this gumby earth
& you with your mother teresa heart
& your cat in the hat smile should know

~the meaning of life lies within you~
dr. albert schweitzer & a kazoo

Dedicated to Patti Smith

LOVE is eternal

you were born and when i first held you
the conversation with your eyes spoke of still water
my promise—a steadfast Father's love you could rely on
to guide and protect you...oh Zion

a man's character is his soul
and son you cannot control money, health, fame
or who will love you—
we only have power over our actions
sacrifice like love, is the only thing that is true
much like virtue

everything in this world is temporal
but LOVE is eternal
LOVE IS ETERNAL!

For my son, Zion William Lamont

walt whitman america

Walt Whitman reciting his poem America as recorded by Thomas Edison. (Public Domain)	Billy Lamont's poetry with Em Kruz of upwordspiral's bluesy hip hop music
America	oh captain, my captain!
Centre of equal daughters, equal sons,	i too sing the body electric!
All, all alike endear'd, grown, ungrown, young or old,	good grey poet
Strong, ample, fair, enduring, capable, rich	i too sing a song of myself
Perennial with the Earth, with Freedom, Law and Love	america... we need an intelligent heart
	a loving mind
	~LOVE, intelligence of the heart
	will light your mind~
	oh captain, my captain
	i too sing the body electric!!!

electric!
electric!
electric!
america...
we need an intelligent heart

a loving mind

~LOVE, intelligence of the
heart

will light your mind~

this is the voice of walt
whitman...

America

Centre of equal daughters,
equal sons,

All, all alike endear'd, grown,
ungrown, young or old,

america...

Strong, ample, fair, enduring,
capable, rich

we need an intelligent
heart!!!

Perennial with the Earth,
with Freedom, Law and Love

a loving mind!!!

imagine a day...

I would like to invite you, the reader, to Imagine A Day. *To take a moment to close your eyes and sit quietly and meditate and intuitively sense your great potential. To take a moment to pray and shake off the dirt of propaganda and mental slavery that sometimes gets on us from the media and in our day to day activities. I would like to invite you to imagine taking a cleansing love bath, to get baptized by light, to get in touch with your soul, with who you really are, with what you are created to be and how you can reform yourself and reform our world with LOVE. I invite you to* Imagine A Day!

imagine a day...
    when children run and play
    with minds that are free
    to think and create
            ...a new day

imagine a day...
    filled with an awe of creation and creator
    the grassy fields, the thunderous oceans,
    the majestic mountains
    my body, my heart and mind
    my soul
    a meditation
    your creation

imagine a day...
    wondrous child
    filled with the acute awareness
    of the love that surrounds us
    and how your love can change the world

imagine a day...
   with an appreciation of all our senses
   alive and awake
   the wonder of seeing eyes
   to hear with hearing ears
   what is the spirit saying?
   i can feel you
   the texture of your touch
   the fragrance and mathematics of this moment
   etched now in my memory
   as i taste such a variety of tastes
   alive and awake

imagine a day...

LOVE
intelligence of the heart
will light your mind

LOVE
intelligence of the heart
will light your mind

imagine a day...
   beautiful child
   when food is served to all the starving and hungry
   when a home is built for the homeless and they can rest
   when war veterans find peace
   when the disabled find healthcare and security
   when orphans and widows find a family and are blessed

imagine a day...
   when you and i
   lay in the grass
   and stare at the sky
   and dream

imagine a day...
   without a glass ceiling
   misleading and stealing
   our potential
   beautiful child
   there is no limit to what you can do with your life!

imagine a day...
   when equality is a reality
   and we can trust in solidarity
   as brothers and sisters

imagine a day...
   filled with hope

imagine a day...
   filled with the realization
   that you have your own fingerprints
   and the knowing
   that there is only one magnificent you!

imagine a day...
   pregnant with love and life
   awakened to the mathematics of every moment

the wondrous gift of today

~at dawn
a new day is born~

*This was written for my son, Zion, and his fifth grade class
on September 30, 2010*

*~Dedicated to the Beatles—the late John Lennon, Paul
McCartney, the late George Harrison and Ringo Starr and also
Yoko Ono~*

like marconi...(epilogue)

at the village dock
the purity of newly fallen snow
alone, I recite this poem to God
and sit in awe of Yahweh in the afterglow

zion william lamont
~holy protecting mountain~

the deeper the tree's root
the greater the spiritual fruit
that springs upward in praise of God!

like marconi...
like marconi sending the first wireless message to sea
heart transmissions bouncing off of holy satellite
when watching the sunrise by the ocean shore
the early morning sings with first light

like marconi...
like marconi sending the first wireless message to sea

sonnet for the sea

the wind whispers with wonder
in seashells i never find
as love screams like thunder
& swims to the shore of my mind

the passion within the ocean fills
kisses, streams of consciousness
as the seed of creation spills
& splashes in your loveliness

the mystery of the mountain
is the light in sunshine
as i bathe naked in your fountain
& drink from your lips of wine

~ your beauty is like the sea
  waves that comfort me ~

I-SISsy

i declare that those in the death cult ISIS
who are terrorizing and murdering
innocent children,
loving women, and virtuous men
now be called by the new name
I-SISsy

Inspired by Dylan Thomas'
X and diamond shaped poems and adding
interior rhymes. ☺
X

billy lamont

politicians   a b u s e   p o w e r
because greed wants to maintain
unfair s o c i a l structure
for   personal   gain
ignorance   rules
when they smear
and fear
youth
enraged
painted black
freedom under
m e d i a a t t a c k
compassion   in   action
casts off big business hex
we   are   not   generation x!!!

protest: a declaration

protest
a declaration
for the strobe light generation

*　　　　　　　　*　　　　　　　　*

in Jah,
Jesus Christ
and his wife, The Holy Spirit
we are one
in body, sight,
spirit, and light

*　　　　　　　　*　　　　　　　　*

we have this dream
that mankind can be a team
and feed the poor
have peace not war

we are activists
and in our hearts we wave a protest sign
that reads, "to be a leader
is to be a servant of mankind"

for violations of human rights
we will demonstrate
and not keep silence
but will not drink the wine of violence
we believe in passive resistance

love,
love, love
shine on
and pretty soon the daggers
will turn to flowers

we would rather suffer in our youth
than live the lie
and if they ask us to compromise the truth
we shout "we would rather die!"

you never look back
when you have your hand to the plow
the future is a field of harvest
the future is now!

we repent for our father's sin
for the blood spilled of the native indian
and the slavery of the african
we feel the pain and persecution of our women
the gays and the lesbian
and will not suffer the abuse of our children
and we will not tolerate not having a voice in our
government
while big business kills our animals
and destroys our land and environment

war on poverty!
we want to heal the poverty
in this country

and poverty can be physical
                    intellectual
                    or spiritual

so if your eyes are a funeral
and you are a haunted house
exorcise the demons
shake the ghosts
shake the ghosts!
there is hope
don't dream in black
don't dream in black
don't dream in black
a serpent and a dove
evil will turn to love

just sit with us
and dine
and we will drink from a chalice
filled with new wine

all those who hunger and thirst
for righteousness
this is our song for you:

    let your heart always stay true
    because a sin or a short coming
    is just an absence of a virtue
    live by love
    and work for justice
    shed light on darkness!

dignity

pride is negative energy

dignity
      & confidence
            is healthy

be humble & follow your dream
& don't let anyone
          ever
            steal your self-esteem!

prejudice: a disease with no vaccine?

nigger, honkey, spick
heinie, guinea, mick
i'm sick and tired of prejudice!

prejudice! a disease with no vaccine?
prejudice! the worst plague ever seen!
prejudice! this world should be quarantined!
prejudice! a wound we've got to clean!

the future takes us back
to our history
to learn
lesson one:

we can kill with the bomb
or a gun
or words filled with deadly poison
from our tongue

degradation
segregation
it's a lack of education!

sticks and stones
will break my bones
but words are deadlier
in the mouth of clones

commie, pollock, spook
red, chink, gook
homo, queer, dyke
wop, hebe, kike

is this what you want me to be?
or is it hype?
is it me you hate?
or your own stereotype?

words ripped from a soul still bleeding

x-ray mind

x-ray mind
taste my thoughts
and tell me
is it the flavor of truth?

environmental terrorism

acid rain
toxic waste
big business greed and neglect
the greenhouse effect

tropical rain forests bulldozed
no conservation
animals murdered by poacher's bullets
wildlife extinction

raping the sky
and waging war on creation
is a sick science fiction movie evolution
you ask me to drink from your fountain of wisdom
and it's water pollution
environmental terrorism

i pray for a revolution of love
i pray for a revolution of hope
militant pacifism

all creation will be one
when the land of my father
is the land for my son

love the sky
make peace with the earth!

Dedicated to Peter Garrett of Midnight Oil

haiku-a-cuckoos too

For Witness—Human Rights Justice Organization founded by Peter Gabriel

freedom of speech, but...
then jailed for your point of view
haiku-a-cuckoo

For Greenpeace—Environmental Justice Organization

misinformation
paints climate change not true blue
haiku-a-cuckoo

worn-out walking stick

a low esteem out of dreams stammer
the fame name vanity glamour

no place to rest my head wishing i had a bed not a funky
thrift store hat
never enough money had too much to eat greedy
gluttony fat cat bureaucrat

a system to beat avoid the heat need food to eat thief
an eloquent speech but out of reach tax relief

got no home get no respect used to neglect funny
it's a lifetime job making sure i don't get robbed acting
like a snob looking after all my money

some may be crazy they say we are all lazy
can't get a break helplessness
make a deal with lawyers who steal with a smile that is
fake good business

in a bad mood too many people are rude
begging for food desperate
love is like rust no one to trust hating the pet regret

no welcome mat diplomat worn-out walking stick
artificial superficial madison avenue slick
any kind is sick homelessness
this type is thick loneliness

underground railroad

On Friday, June 26, 2010, as I was writing this poem at Robert Moses State Park beach, on the boardwalk at Field 5, on Long Island, NY, a small Cessna airplane made an emergency crash landing, with the plane bouncing and stopping twelve feet away and facing me. The airplane stopped three feet from the boardwalk, and I was the only person standing on the boardwalk. I also was the first responder to the airplane to help the pilot. This poem was completed during breakfast on July 5th, twenty minutes before it was recorded in one take, with all the other tracks for my spoken word CD entitled Outlaw Of Love. *This is a true story, and this event was on the evening news on television and in newspapers. An airplane literally made a crash landing into the writing of this poem!*

my reputation and life's work
was ruthlessly gunned down in cold blood
...but under the radar, in the backstreets
my character, my soul is still alive!

the media creating heroes to later destroy them
it's my child and home and not the state's!
people bought wholesale and then sold retail by companies
are we citizens or consumers to the government?

entrapment never worked with me
i'm too illuminated, you see?
so i'm framed
named
blamed
and shamed
in corporate greed's deadly game

gossip rags and blogs
try to say, "i'm crazy"
then pressure my friends
the means does not justify their ends

"people get ready
The Lord is coming"
like an abolitionist forced into hiding
now i'm riding the underground railroad

proclaim liberty to the prisoners
proclaim liberty!
you can't imprison me
for following Jesus The Christ!
The Lord has already set me free

proclaim liberty and be a helping hand
to the orphans, the widows, the poor, the young, the elderly
and the handicapped
worthlessly trapped
in credit card slavery

this poetry ripped out of my soul still bloody
these memories have been removed with surgery
Jesus, you know me intimately
Lord, i love you very deeply

~like an outlaw of love
forced into hiding
i'm riding the underground railroad~

the feeling of the earth beneath my bare feet
the sound of the ocean at twilight
her fragrance and the way she looks in that summer dress
the rumble of a motorcycle
icy cold beer and american rock and roll
bless my soul

i have just come from a funeral
alone, standing on this boardwalk
leaning on a railing
and writing this poem
praying about life and death
praying about the direction of my life
and that the remainder of my life
can be as fruitful
and as pleasing to GOD as possible
and then listening quietly
listening for God's reply—
a still soft voice in my heart
but instead i hear
crowds of beach goers shouting,
"watch out! get out of the way!!!"
i turn to face a small plane falling from the sky—
a crash landing and the plane bounces towards me
and stops twelve feet away and facing me

run!
run to aid the 89-year-old world war II veteran pilot from the plane
he's alive
run for freedom

felt like he entered the warmth of my peaceful, intimate
prayer

salvation
redemption
divine intervention
and freedom
~freedom like the 4th of july~

ideals and what is real

searching, searching for the truth
turning round and round just like a wheel
the soul is a spiritual mirror
deciding what is and isn't real

everyone reaches for their dream
looking to an ideal
life is a balance beam
deciding what is and isn't real

moods and attitudes
ideals and what is real

worry 666

wor.ry is chok/ing me
and weav/ing me a mask
of in/se.cu/ri.ty

house of mirrors: are you making love to me?

is it a visual image?
or is it a mirage?
a mystery
the alchemy of our chemistry

are you making love to me?
or what i seem to be?
are you making love to me?
or what you want me to be?

house of mirrors, house of mirrors

am i here?
or really over there?
a blanketed circle in a square
find me if you dare!
find me if you really care!

house of mirrors, house of mirrors

are you making love to me?
or what i seem to be?
are you making love to me?
or what you want me to be?

house of mirrors, house of mirrors

mask of comedy/mask of tragedy
house of mirrors, house of mirrors

will i look different
in another light?
under all this extreme pressure
for another day and night?

is this reality?
or what i seem to be?
is this really me?
or what you dream me to be?

house of mirrors, house of mirrors

vanity/vanity/vanity
my world is a reflection of me

house of mirrors, house of mirrors

i fully face and trace the surface of the smooth, clean glass
that blurs the boundary of reality
the mirror's reflection creates a new perception of what is
truth and light
until i turn, and walk, and slam full force into the spiritual
mirror glass
the glass is unbreakable but my heart is shattered and i am
bleeding

~my heart of broken glass~

house of mirrors
house of mirrors

flattery 666

words slit skin sub/tl/y
bleed/ing deep con.vic/tion
flat/ter.y's in.ten.tion

emotional vampires

emotional vampires
suck your blood
drain your soul
feed off of your—

desire
your naked beauty
lies on the bed
wrapped in barbed wire

you say,
"don't tell me who i am
& what i am—

feeling"
a spirit shrieks in the night
desperate
for healing

"i know what it is like to be dead"
i said
long ago remembering
remembering
if a baby is not held it will die
& so i lie
holding myself & admiring you
until i whisper
"true agape love please ignite the—

fire"
on fire
with spiritual love & carnal animal lust
until skin is punctured by the rose's briar

        the pure white sheets now run blood red
        & i am left alone

needing
my soul lies bleeding

a distraction can lead to a deception can lead to
destruction from emotional vampires

hungry ghost

the subtleties of persuasion
the evil of manipulation
a kiss before a betrayal
your seduction is corruption

a kiss before a betrayal
black lipstick kiss to my soul
it's all about control
isn't it?

there's a famine in our heart
a hungry ghost trying to feast
on a spiritual pride
that only rots us from the inside
as this friendly decay
feeds another angry skeleton—
content to be a victim
hungry ghost, hungry ghost

you dried the long stemmed roses
hung them upside down over our bed
should have known it was a symbol
of your absence of love
a doorway to the dead

oh, Lord deliver us
there's a famine in our heart
a hungry ghost trying to feast
on a spiritual pride
that only rots us from the inside
as this friendly decay

feeds another angry skeleton—
content to be a victim
hungry ghost, hungry ghost

romanticized death
stealing my breath

when will flesh appear on ezekiel's dry bones?
the hungry ghost, the hungry ghost
need to eat the bread of life
taste holy communion

Jesus, by your precious blood
just broke the spell of satan
shined a light on the shadowy phantom
with The Holy Ghost
just cast away a tormenting demon
with The Holy Ghost
The Holy Ghost, The Holy Ghost

ignorance > stigma < alive mystical

~when ignorance is not bliss
it can get dangerous
you see it in serial killer lamentations
graffitied in faces at subway stations~

i've got a stigma
attached to my taboo
but i was framed
i never did it, it's not true
it's all a big lie
you brainless, soulless fascist
Fuck You!

martin luther nailing the ninety-five theses
to the church door
holy radicals declare this a sacred space
when we love it's like we are spitting
in the devil's face

balance the alive mystical
with the pure theological
the spiritual
not religion
the gift of a vision
of sweet Jesus

shadow box

who murdered me?
she's sleeping in my bed
pulled out all of my hair
cursed my head

you're threatening to cut off my feet
leave me an amputee
want to gash out my eyes
to make sure that I don't see

like a relic you try to place me in your memory box
...shadow box

in the cathedral the dove flies
but crashes into the stained glass ceiling
now you want to clip his wings
you open sewer
plotting in darkness, devoid of any feeling

Christianity is greater than
the dogma of a poisoned mind
you try to gash out my eyes
to make sure that I am blind

very unkind

you want the blood of a new saint
you hand me a brush, but only allow one color of paint
you secretly drug me up, but my heart won't faint
i'm breaking out of this shadow box
shadow box, shadow box

the difference between knowledge and wisdom
the distance between seeing and vision

the closed coffin is now an open treasure chest
where the Spirit of the Lord is there is freedom

you want the blood of a new saint
you hand me a brush, but only allow one color of paint
you secretly drug me up, but my heart won't faint
i'm breaking out of this shadow box
shadow box, shadow box

original_negative [the power to dream]

as cruelty, manipulation, brainwashing
and conditioning
plot irreverence for life
compete for my misery
i must get to the essence of true thought
the heart of an idea
and then add hope

-we have the power to dream-

Heaven is weeping red tear droplets tonight
crashing thunder sobbing
on surreal blue skies
will the earth be cleansed?
will the poor soul be avenged?
as i bleed upon the machine

sweat stinging my eyes
the pain is becoming too much
-survival-
my emotions turn off like the pop of a switch
when a circuit is overloaded—the fuse is blown!
i can no longer feel anything
there's poison water flowing in these pipes
i remember memorizing you and all your beautiful
features and ways
the original_negative is now scratched
i can't even remember you!

i have seen where the conveyor belt leads to
in this death factory
alienation—speaking to me of broken lifetimes

feel like a fly trapped on the screen door
waiting for the moment to fly for the sky
the chrome metallic sky
still grasping for the substance of hope
a dream within my vision
written on the fleshly tablets of my heart
-we hold the power to dream-
to dream of something better, of a better life
the resources all around us that they don't consider
that they cannot even see
~awaiting imagination to give birth to holy idea~

feel like a fly trapped on the screen door
waiting for the moment to fly for the sky
the chrome metallic sky
still grasping for the substance of hope
a dream within my vision
written on the fleshly tablets of my heart
-we hold the power to dream-
to dream of something better, of a better life
the resources all around us that they don't consider
that they cannot even see!

~awaiting imagination to give birth to holy idea~

WE HAVE THE POWER TO DREAM!!!

inspired by luke haughwout of heart of darkness

universeheartgracelifewonder

imperfect pearl buried in the mud trash sin dirt touch
the Jah sapphire sky star shine above taste golden
forgiveness repentance joy liquid fire anointing oil electric
shock flame of the Spirit that washes away all that is not
love creation you sealed with compassion glow sacrifice
kiss authority mercy blood unconditional gentle hug
comfort salvation baptism

universeheartgracelifewonder

~yesterday today forever
incubate Jesus diamond peace~

dirty dishes

issues piling up like dirty dishes
that were busy serving up trauma
this wandering, gypsy heart
is still looking for a home, momma

intimacy problems wears a new dress
real love traveling your way
disconnect, repossess
should have loved you more/should have loved you less

a homemade meal made from a recipe
filled with broken promises
i'm writing to try and express the pain
in a run-on sentence without a comma
this faithful heart is homeless, momma

the pot heating on the stove
with the lid on it
will always boil faster
loving you is like speeding down the highway in a $500 car
trying not to get killed by a natural disaster

one day you came home to me
in a whirlwind of your usual stress
you said, "don't ask any questions
just listen, i ask your forgiveness
i brought shame on you
i confess"

she felt the embrace of grace
and looked into the eyes of forgiveness
should have loved you more/should have loved you less

a home is not a house or money
a home is the love and acceptance of a family
what happens when a wife does not leave
and cleave to her husband?
when her husband is not part of her family
while she states "family values" at church
and in the community merely to impress?
should have loved you more/should have loved you less

time to clean up your kitchen
you think to change
is to sanitize and escape
so you change your hair, clothes, apartment, and your job
buy a new car
go for fine dining in a martini bar
buy a new home
move to a new location
take a fancy vacation
escape to find a place with the exact same situation

while you and the church elders
judge the artist
you call me a "weirdo" every day
they say i'm "eccentric"
without hearing a word i say
they tell me, "you can't newly create
don't innovate!
until we've finished this debate
until she's in a perfect state
forget about the homeless
the widows
the orphans

the disabled
the blind
the war veterans
the poor
go shopping in the store!!!
have dinner with a new friend
who is an unenlightened bore
go shopping in the store
make sure the rich are safe and secure
and they will open to you a new door"

free spirit versus ambition
that is selfish
should have loved you more/should have loved you less

I have to say at church you put on a pretty good show
in private you were cruel and never even kind
no one will ever know/no one will ever know
with every spiritual seed uprooted
it is impossible to grow

slashing tongue finds an easy temper
unrealistic selfish demands smashing
against my self-esteem
you tried but you can't destroy every spiritual dream

every day you treated your husband
like the kitchen garbage
it's like you threw your treasure out with the trash
like you gave me all your sins and debts
while you secretly swiped the cash

i tried to get us help, counseling
to get to the essence of the issues
that we needed to address
in a situation far too complex
should have loved you more/should have loved you less

you are so cruel
can't even talk to you
have to keep silence
as you dictate your contradictions
and try to manipulate situations
as I'm stranded here trying to clean up the mess
should have loved you more/should have loved you less

you tried entrapment and lies
to steal our son
and tried to destroy my character
and life's work
with one explosive bomb
that didn't work
did you sacrifice our son's well-being in the process?
You got your man with muscles
and your new house
congratulations on your new success!
Should have loved you more/should have loved you less

I tried to define for you the difference
between joy and happiness
should have loved you more
should have loved you less

free spirit versus ambition

that is selfish
should have love you more—with a heart more pure
should have loved you less—without inheriting your
crushing debts

my prayer for you—
~leave with my blessing
God has immeasurable grace
hope you meet Jesus's genuine Holy Spirit face-to-face
the letter of the law kills
but The Spirit gives life
and you were never my wife~

trapped turtles

this morning my son zion said,
"cars are like trapped turtles in parking spots"
i replied, "they certainly are. good observation, son."
and then took him inside to have a new york bagel

hedge of thorns [trash can noise hiccup]

beat up, bruised and swollen
can't even keep track of what's been stolen

trashed down, smashed up
trash can noise with a hiccup

i need a hedge of thorns surrounding me
a hedge of thorns, a hedge of thorns
i pray a hedge of thorns

razor cut, sweat and blood
playing around in the mud

black eye, fat lip
sexy girl in leather with a whip

i need a hedge of thorns surrounding me
a hedge of thorns, a hedge of thorns
i pray a hedge of thorns

beat up, bruised and swollen
everything I have ever had has been stolen

trashed down, smashed up
trash can noise with a hiccup

black eye, fat lip
sexy girl looking at me wants to strip

i need a hedge of thorns surrounding me
a hedge of thorns, a hedge of thorns
i pray a hedge of thorns

beat up, smashed down
can't find any love in this town
beat up, smashed down
semen stains on her wedding gown
a big joke in this town

need change, shaking a cup?
broken nose and a hiccup

beat down, throwing up
trash can noise with a hiccup

i need a hedge of thorns surrounding me
a hedge of thorns, a hedge of thorns
i pray a hedge of thorns

whiskey shots, cheap cigars
cigarette smoke, fast cars
tabs in all the pubs and bars
all my friends are like movie stars
all my friends are like movie stars!

new hat, cool tattoo
it's what makes you, You

con artists without any wit
not going to take your shit!!!

tattoos, good booze, new blues
gospel music like the sunday news!!!!!!!

i need a hedge of thorns surrounding me
a hedge of thorns, a hedge of thorns
i pray a hedge of thorns

i need a hedge of thorns
surrounding me
a hedge of thorns
 a hedge of thorns
i pray a hedge of thorns

She's Got PMS!

I tried being sensitive
I am being really sweet
I gave her an entire box of her favorite chocolates
but only standing here in defeat

She's got PMS! I'm feeling a lot of stress!
She's got PMS! She's feeling so depressed!
She's got PMS! I'm feeling so oppressed!
She's got PMS! I better buy her that new dress!

Is this hormones?
It happens the same day every month
I better make plans to play poker with my buddies
She's spitting death from her sexy lips
She's sitting on the floor crying
As she's eating potato chips
It seems like she is dying!
Or will kill me...
during this Pre-Minstrel Syndrome!
Is this due to a hormone?

She's got PMS! I'm feeling my death in her caress!
She's got PMS! I'm going down with my last breath!
She's got PMS!
i didn't do anything wrong
but she's forcing me to confess!
She's got PMS! I'm under a lot of duress!
She's got PMS!
She's choking me
and I'm caressing my last breath!
She's got PMS!
I better buy gushy tushy a new dress!!!

Larry Norman

*For my beloved close personal friend, the late Larry Norman, who
believed in me as a pioneering performance poet and who was
backing me by having me open some shows for him and planning
to record a full album for me as one of his artists on a new version
of his legendary Solid Rock Records in 1998–2000. When Larry
Norman's health failed in 2001, we had only recorded for a few hours
in a NY recording studio after a show we did that I organized at The
Knitting Factory as a benefit for Jubilee 2000. The tapes from that
recording session went missing in his archives vault shortly after.
When Larry Norman's health failed, I did everything in my power
to help him get the money he needed for emergency healthcare.
This is the poem I wrote and recited to make a plea for emergency
healthcare for Larry Norman as I opened the show for The
Alarm at Cornerstone Festival 2004 and is a true representation
of the Larry Norman I knew and of his GREAT SPIRIT!!!*

~Larry Norman...brave innovator, ghetto street preacher,
visionary pioneer, brilliant songwriter, a personality with an
amazing sense of humor, a hand reaching to Heaven with a
pointed finger, vineyard church co-founder, illuminated Holy
Bible teacher, mystical revelator, holy reformer, Christian
rock and roll father, a Jesus The Christ follower!...my west
coast brother...a blond ray from the sun~

u2

minimal notes reverberate
delay and rise to Heaven
like praises before God's throne
swirling guitar blasts for justice
driving rhythms of jubilee
light arises in the darkness
love casting the demons away from me
The Spirit that upholds life
given voice
gloria!
rejoice!
a voice
bono vox
a voice
vocalized breath
distinct notes of pure passion
one voice
a voice of the people
a voice of compassion
kindred spirits looking real cool
dressed up in postmodern fashion
u2
sheep in wolves clothing usher in a mystical communion

For Bono, The Edge, Larry Mullen Jr., and Adam Clayton

times square billboard

~don't pollute yourself with porn
your eye is a gate
a door
keep it pure
don't be pornography's whore

advertising that is subliminal
conditioning that is criminal
sex sells
and sex smells
so buy our products!~

dippin' in the chromosome jar

uptown, in a high-class bar
now your dreams revealed
you want to be a rock-and-roll star!

not callous or as hard
now your hands are shakin'
and can only reach as far...
as the chromosome jar!

dippin' in the chromosome jar
dippin' in, dippin' in
dippin' in the chromosome jar
dipping in the chromosome jar-ar

gender blender, gender blender
you've turned on the gender blender

your pants, shiny and so nice
now boys come to see you
the girls no longer look twice!

you don't have to sashay gay
to be a rock star
and your hand can only reach as far...
as the chromosome jar!

dippin' in the chromosome jar
dippin' in, dippin' in
dippin' in the chromosome jar
dipping in the chromosome jar-ar

sexual, changed to bi, bye
now Y changed to X, why?
your ex wants to know why, why?
you used to be such a macho guy!

gender blender, gender blender
you have put your manhood in the gender blender

dippin' in the chromosome jar
dippin' in, dippin' in
dippin' in the chromosome jar
dipping in the chromosome jar-ar

potential 666

al.ways a la/zy day
a waste of po.ten.tial
pay the bill for e/vil

The Woman (She Don't Care)

She's mommy's baby
She's daddy's little princess
Or so I am told
But the feelings are growing
The book is unfolding
How could she lose what she possibly owned?

The sexy young woman
Will merge with her lover
She is easily led
But a young man's passions will move to another
Gently persuaded to other beds

The middle aged woman
With many a lover
Sits alone in her chair
Revitalizing, she covers with makeup
Secretly pulling gray hairs from her head

She don't care about tenderness
She don't care about life's loving bliss
She don't care, her love has turned to lust
She don't care

The poor old woman
With no one to love her
Sleeps alone in her bed
No one is calling
Her life is now falling
No one cares if she's dead

She don't care about tenderness
She don't care about life's loving bliss
She don't care, her love has turned to lust
She don't care, her love has turned to dust
She don't care

Inspired by the music of Nick and Rich DiStasi

dr. dino

dr. dino is suffering from fanny burps
with an exquisite aftertaste

can you believe evolution?

"children, children
darwin, you and me
descended from a tree
descended from a big hairy monkey"

they teach you fact
that is not even proven
break their own scientific laws
with evolution

since when is theory truth?
since when do we corrupt our youth?
keep an open mind, keep an open mind
can't let the blind lead the blind
lead the blind
is a theory a solution?
can you believe evolution?

"children, children
a smelly fish jumped up out of the sea
grew arms and legs
and became you and me"

has man ever created anything better than himself
or does he kill with his pollution
while breaking every scientific law
with evolution

since when is theory truth?
since when do we corrupt our youth?
keep an open mind, keep an open mind

can't let the blind lead the blind
lead the blind
is a theory a solution?
can you believe evolution?

maybe it makes you feel better
thinking this is all just one big accident
and that those who survive are most fit
but are you losing your sense of humanity with it?

maybe when you think that only the strong survive
it steals your love for other people
it steals your reason for being alive

maybe it makes you feel less responsible
less accountable
for decisions you have made
while secretly hoping past deeds will fade
and you will not have to stand on
feeble foundations you have laid

or maybe
you
and charles darwin
are just looking
for a license
to sin

i went searching for the missing link
and found out this theory really does stink
what evolved first the flower or the bee?
and what is the history of energy?

how can you have a reaction without an action?
and what about the law of entropy?
how can you have a creation without a creator?
and why does matter not have any past eternity?

so give God the glory
for the human body
with its beauty
and complexity

each of a million optic nerves
must find their mate simultaneously
in order for a newborn baby
to see

and what should he see?

God's glory
in life's rich design
God's glory in this world's harmony
and interdependency

so give God the glory
it actually takes more faith
to believe in evolution
than in creation

can you believe evolution?

unborn babies

unborn babies
cry out from the womb
in another dimension
weeping the words—
"i was knitted into the womb
of my mother
by the loving hand of GOD
my head was crushed
by the grotesque hand of man
murdered before even born
we are crying
crying
the lives we never lived
the loves we never loved
the creations left uncreated
we never felt the warmth of being held
of a smile
of a homemade meal
never felt the love
of a family or a friend
oh, the lives we never lived
all that is left is a ghost"

with the flicker of a candle
i caught a glimpse of eternity
saw a glitter of light
from a womb for unborn souls
overflowing with the colors of new life

Inspired by Director Scott Perry filming an episode of In Fear Of *web series in my Victorian House apartment in Babylon, NY— Thursday, March 15, 2012.*

Uncle Ned

you told me, "this bloody crucifixion
has the most beautiful flourishing resurrection"
i didn't believe you
now i have to find you
the rusted lock unbolted
the prison cell doors swing open
outside into bright, heated sunlight
so this is first light
i now remember what sunlight feels like on my face
warms me as the camera of my eye
goes out of focus and dissolves into
the sun of new life

Dedicated to my Uncle Ned Kavanaugh. This poem was written in a burst of inspiration that felt like dictation on May 3, 2005, at 3:30 p.m. at Starbucks, Commack, NY. I received a call a few minutes later from my cousin Kevin Kavanaugh to say Uncle Ned passed on into eternity just then at 3:32 p.m.

your lame lukewarm leprosy love (went whimpering away)

where are you now, love
when i need you in this ambulance?
your lame lukewarm leprosy love
went whimpering away—

i am standing here crying
my love is dying
kicking and screaming

where are you, love
in this emergency?
i've got this lame lukewarm leprosy love
that went whimpering away—
lame lukewarm leprosy love
likes to sleep alone
lame lukewarm leprosy love
don't like to talk on the phone
likes to be satisfied
or groan
a co-dependent moan
or leave town
this bird has flown

i'm sensitive and true
unlike you
you are abusive
your love is toxic
so why don't you spit your vindictive poison
somewhere else

i don't want your
lame lukewarm leprosy love
fare thee well, my ill
and leave me alone
this bird has flown

you don't speak the five languages of love
where were the words of affirmation,
acts of service,
gift giving,
quality time
and physical touch?

your love was hexed
i'll no longer be vexed
loved you much too much
you are abusive
your love is toxic
so spit your vindictive poison somewhere else

where are you now, love
when i need you in this ambulance?
your lame lukewarm leprosy love
went whimpering away—
your lame lukewarm leprosy love
somehow went astray
your lame lukewarm leprosy love
went limping away!

poison fruit

intelligent minds see things in symbols
i know you long enough to know your patterns
and wise enough to know what is coming next—

your small town playhouse drama
conceived in your immature and dark mind
will bear poison fruit of trauma

if there is fruit, what is the root?
trauma can be healed with LOVE and wisdom
patterns can be changed with thoughtfulness
recognize the toxic weed of your actions
and dig up the root
plant a healthy seed
and bear better fruit
of new LIFE

if there is fruit
what is the root?

the futility of love

the futility of love
today i feel very different, so—
it's a van gogh morning on this scummy earth!
love is futile
when trusting someone with no self-worth
who counterfeits new birth

love is futile
even crossing a tumultuous sea with love's sincerity
love is futile
when wearing your heart out filled with loyalty
love is futile
you bother me
love is futile
i have to say you disgust me
& are scuzzy
love is futile
lifetime of work has dehumanized me!

love is futile
when you are a faithful man of integrity
and an outstanding father
and you lose your life's work
to a less than faithful ex
sure feels like unknowingly trusting
in an evil witch's hex
love is futile

love is futile
when your life's work has been stolen
in an outdated court system
with a judge presiding

who is really a politician
whose stench
will finally later
get him kicked off the bench
love is futile

love is futile
when you have to find a way to live
by this false judge's thoughtless,
bureaucratic, arrogant decisions
love is futile
& filled with conditions
& contradictions
love is futile

love is futile
when you fight and have won
joint custody of your son
but lose your life's work
& are rewarded with—
getting two hours of sleep a day
after working through the night
for ten years now
& with still more to come?
this way
you can travel forty minutes each way
to be with your son
to do homework with him
& be a real father to him every day?
but still needing to pay
20% child support to an ex

so she can pay for the new house
that she bought with the money stolen
from your retirement plan
so she can make a new life with her new man?
and I was awarded with the privilege to pay
the lawyers and government with the $30,000
from what remained from my retirement plan?
as all the while i was the one providing
my son's daily needs of food, clothes, sneakers
while the state and federal government had the gall
to take an additional 35% of my salary
in elevated income taxes for the bureaucracy?
It's like being shaken down
by a government mafia of the greedy
love is futile

love is futile
& all the while i stayed strong
& kept a smile
as all i could possibly do was work
to hopefully possibly pay
for elevated gas prices
to travel to care for my son
& he would live with me whenever I was off from work
& when he was off from school
& during the summer
it was my joy to sacrifice my life
so my son could have a better life
i didn't have any of the money necessary
but had outstanding credit
i had no time to sleep

no time to date for seven years
or for poetry
i was grateful to be alive
& somehow i would survive
sometimes i could steal a few minutes for nature's beauty
or to listen to a song everyday
and to pray
and remain joyful
as i work and work and work
without much help or even a break
living on adrenaline, coffee,
and occasional mini cigars
when i found an unhealthy moment to breathe
love is futile
while i keep getting promoted and promoted
with more responsibilities
and couldn't even break even on my budget each month
for bare necessities
all the while getting in crushing debt each month
like i told the unjust judge would happen
and he replied, "just do it
or i will throw you in jail
you son of a bitch"
sure feels like being lorded over
by the rich
love is futile!

love is futile
but i am blessed with survival
until i get laid off from being a manager
at a huge successful company

& i have to laugh because the reason they gave me is
i am making too much money
& the company justifies it by blaming their greed
on the economy
love is futile
at first it made me strong
but finally breaks my back financially
love is futile
you can't live life without any money
or time for yourself
love is futile
when caught up in paperwork and process
love is futile
when the money machine calls my name
love is futile
body thumping
thrown under another bus
love is futile with every injustice

the american dream is a lie
when the promise of prosperity
ends in bankruptcy
love is futile
when you don't have the heart or spirit to kill
or to do ill
to take revenge
upon those who have tried to murder me
when you are given the chance
over and over again
love is futile
when the corporate asses line up that you just won't kiss

love is futile
when you refuse to taste of their senseless excess
love is futile
when you get kicked off the ladder of success!
love is futile
the american dream sure was a great idea
before it was co-opted by big business!
love is futile
& life sure is not bliss
when enslaved and chained to a cookie cutter cubicle
abyss
& forced to be a good consumer and buy and buy and buy
to perhaps survive
love is futile
when the american dream is a lie!

love is futile
i wonder how many presidents of corporations
or unjust judges
or bureaucratic politician memes
have ever had the ruthless greedy
come to steal their dreams?
or have they ever been up through the night
without any food for their hunger pains?
or enough heat to battle the winter's frigid temperatures?
or without an umbrella when it rains?
with just clothes with holes and stains?
all because you love your son
and want to be a real father to him
after being thrown away like garbage from both
your ex

& big business
love is futile!

love is futile!
you have zero understanding of me
love is futile
how can you look me in the eyes
and only see
a distortion of me?
i've been blessed with persecution for my faith
demasculinized for my purity of heart
& free mind
been criticized
& marginalized
for my sensitivity
& tolerance for all people
for my holy dignity
& for honoring all life
that was my reward
for all my LOVE—
heart and soul
innovation
& creativity
love is futile!!!

love is futile
when you are rising like a phoenix from the ashes
& then a businessman pretends to love your artwork
to try and pick your pocket for personal gain
love is futile
when a socialite chases you to find fame

it can be like poison in your brain
love is futile
when you were sleeping next to someone narcissistic vain
love is futile
i shower and shower
and bathe
and wash and wash
but just can't wash your skuzz off of me and
get your sleaze to wash down the drain
love is futile
when you are bleeding
and you can't take the pain!!!

love is futile
when you bear your soul to strangers
voice bleeding into a microphone
for their benefit
and they can't even remember billy lamont is your fucking
name!!!
love is futile!!!

love is futile
when the faceless one is stalking you
and tries to allure you
& when he can't he has you framed
love is futile
when you can't prove it
and don't know who is to blame

love is futile
have you ever prayed and worked through the night,

night after night after night
and then by midday
as you pray and pray and pray and pray
the blessings never came?
the blessings are never for today
but always will come another day
love is futile!!!

love is futile
saved up all my love
for love that came
and came and came
but never arrived
love is futile

love is futile
when you listen
as they talk and talk
and talk and talk
and then they don't listen to a single word you say
and then have the nerve to complain
love is futile

love is futile
when you work and work and work and work
and walk and walk and walk
in the pounding rain
just to be with them
and then when you arrive
they greet you with disdain
love is futile!

love is futile...
love is futile...
except when greeted by the kindness
of genuine friendship
& you unexpectedly shake the hand of its generosity
as you are looking into the eyes of sincerity
love is futile...
except when love is the glue of a loving family
love is futile...
except when bonding with a newborn baby
love is futile...
except when making and keeping a wedding vow
except when making genuine love on a honeymoon
& being in the moment now
love is futile...
except when praying in the holy of holies
with Father YHWH and Lord JESUS
& when THE HOLY SPIRIT bears witness
& when keri and me
find TRUE LOVE
blessed intimacy
when keri, zion, and me
become a new family
love is not futile!

love is futile...
except when healing body, mind, and soul
love is futile...
except when feeling and actualizing forgiveness
and regaining self-control
love is futile...

except when setting the captives free
from bondage and slavery
with no more worry
with no more anxiety
when no longer wounded or angry
it all dissolves into LOVE's prosperity
love is no longer futile!!!
when the fruit of free will
chooses freedom, tolerance, and liberty
love is no longer futile
when joy arrives and is my strength
like healing oil poured on a wound
love is not futile!
with JESUS
and when THE HOLY SPIRIT bears witness
of the truth
and brings justice!

sad, how i got used to trauma
thinking i was strong like a soldier
i just thought this is what it is like
to be a man of love, a survivor
then staring into the face of the futility of love
& drinking whiskey with a longtime friend
and inspiration
there it is—
like a gift from GOD
a revelation!!!
my life and words are like a blues song
or like a psalm in THE HOLY BIBLE!
staring into the face of the futility of love

& drinking whiskey with a longtime friend
and inspiration
his words and LOVE
and presence
sparkled in his eyes
& within the chemistry of our interaction
& the genius of our conversation
there it is—
a gift from GOD
a revelation!!!
& now
staring into the face of the futility of love
knowing PEACE and JOY
and LOVE is an everyday process
i experienced a KNOWING
you and I can heal
& reach new heights
make new conditioning
with thoughtfulness
& be ever growing—
we can renew our mind
reboot our body
with the frequency of energy
restore GOD's dna
re-image our memory

LOVE is not futile!
LOVE is eternal!
apathy or empathy?
the material or the spiritual?
the only thing in this world that is beyond entropy

the only thing in this world that is not temporal
is LOVE!!!
LOVE IS ETERNAL!!!!!!!!

The TRUTH will still speak
~LOVE, the only thing in this world
that is beyond entropy
and ETERNAL~

*This poem was inspired during a great conversation I had with Dave
Sharp of The Alarm, as we were hanging out and drinking Irish whiskey
in Manchester, England, in January 2014*

teardrop collector

teardrop collector
the tears of joy i am weeping
you are saving and keeping
tears, the melting ice of my facade
your REAL LOVE is a gift from GOD

JESUS IS

JESUS IS
divinity
wrapped in humanity

winter

the white within the snow
is pure and deep
but how long until the
warmth of spring, my love?

puppets in the park

here i stand
left of center
with the future underground
experience is my mentor

social homicide
is emotional suicide
where freedom of choice
has no voice

i won't sell my mind into slavery
i won't be a prisoner to the masses
my eyes can see
i don't need glasses

there are too many puppets in the park
there are too many
puppets in the park

tradition versus change
the normal versus the strange

there's a war going on in my mind
but i've signed a treaty
and in my diary
i saw a message through the graffiti

i'm the artist living on extremes
as the poet in me dreams

i don't subscribe to your personal grief
i won't give in to the master thief
i'm a martyr every day
dying
dying
dying for my beliefs
i'm a martyr
every day dying
       dying
       dying
dying for my beliefs

there are too many
puppets in the park
there are too many puppets
in the park

did you know that some of the rich
seek to control the poor
want a one world government
at your grocery store?

globalization

swipe for food
swipe for gas
and to travel
we have e-z pass

companies downsize
and destroy good people's lives
to make an even bigger profit
and offer great rewards to vice presidents
willing to be fascist

swipe for food
swipe for gas
and to travel
we have e-z pass

i won't take the mark of the beast
i'll be at the Lamb's wedding feast
you have ears to hear
now hear it:
you can beat me
you can jail me
you can torture me
you can shoot me
you can kill the body
but you cannot kill THE HOLY SPIRIT!

Dedicated to the late poet and peace activist Daniel Berrigan

revelation

the book of revelation
is about to unfold
but you cannot buy a stairway to heaven
with fool's gold

i know the Lord JESUS is coming back
i just don't know when
i'm just like daniel
sitting in the lion's den

doug kinney and the sons of jubal singing,
"where are you going to run
in a world without a border?
watch out!!!...here comes the new world order!!!"

did you know the new world order
wants to break the back of the middle class
and topple the world's economy
so they can introduce their fascist cashless society?

the coming new world order
is a prophet daniel
and apostle john prophecy
and by the way
we are currently
a 95% cashless society
one in which a good economy
means more than morality

we love you
it's convenient

it's easy
you are a good citizen
if you greet change
with apathy
but if you oppose us
you are an enemy
to society

we love you
we can control crime
let us straighten out this mess
don't stand in the way of progress

the new world order
are powerful elites
the illuminati
and their secret society
they want to incubate their disease
so they can control the world
with their remedy
this is not a conspiracy theory!
this is reality!!!

in america
in 1980
the georgia guidestones
were built outside of atlanta
stating the new world order intentions
of the powerful elites
the illuminati
and their secret society

to maintain the world with a population
under 500 million people
when there is almost 8 billion souls
in our worldwide family!

the new world order is proposing a genocide
and who will live or die?
only they—the fascist privileged will decide
is this why big pharma
has poison in the vaccines for your baby?
and in our prescription medicines especially for the elderly?
is this why monsanto has poisoned our food
and made it toxic?
this is more demonic
and sinister than greed
and much, much more tragic!!!

the new world order also proposes
they lord over us
with a one world government
and they want to introduce a one world religion
along with their demonic 10 commandments
paving the way for an anti-christ spirit and ruler
and they will sell it all to us through their disaster
and then give us the answer
their false peace

in 1994
meetings in germany
computers, microchips, and
all the latest technology

it was decided that the best place
for a micro-chip in a human would be
in your hand
or forehead
it can be implanted with a hypodermic needle
and with a scanner be easily read
the heat or lithium in your body
can recharge it's battery

these micro-chips are the size of a grain of rice
are these miniature electronic ticks
the mark of the beast?
some say barcodes are encoded with
the number six hundred sixty six

we are in the last days
hear the trumpet sound
with the internet
language no longer confounds

so i'm praising the Lord JESUS
at jericho's wall
as this tower of babel
is starting to fall

i'm worshiping the Lord JESUS
with the music in my poetry
i'm praising the Lord
can you hear the sweet melody?

we now have compatibility

with radio frequency
with mac and pc
worldwide support
not different agendas
because of the global economy
we also have speed of information
and security
and what better way to control
gas, food, travel
all the necessities?

the love of money
the tyranny of the wealthy
the power of the masked secret society
the masons
the illuminati
the kkk
the kgb
the fbi
al-qaeda
the cia

the g8, imf, the world bank
isis

it's time for fasting
and for prayer
for spiritual warfare

my prayers have always
taken me to God's throne

i pray this pilgrim's progress
will soon be raptured and taken home

Jesus Christ is coming back
you better hear the trumpets' sound
this day like joshua
we're standing on holy ground

he who lives by the sword
shall die by the sword
truth comes like a lion
Jesus is Lord!

you ask me, "what's my motivation?"
the great commission
to preach the gospel of Jesus Christ
to every nation

israel is ready to rebuild the temple
false prophet
the anti-christ
the false promise of peace
the anti-christ sits on the throne in the temple
desecration of the temple
abomination of desolation
a new world order
a one world government
one world religion
in reality
satanic spirituality
an anti-christ tyranny

on may 15, 1948
the rebirth of israel
as was foretold by the prophets
isaiah and ezekiel

in the last days just like today
according to the prophet daniel
there would be an increase
in knowledge and travel

for the first time
there is a military highway
to israel
across the south of china
tibet, afghanistan
and pakistan
and with a newly built dam
an asian army can now cross
the river euphrates
for the first time in history
this fulfills the apostle john's prophecy

where it is we are going
only time will tell
you down at the crossroads
don't take the highway to hell

the road is straight
and narrow is the gate
that leads to life
at armageddon
like sodom and gomorrah

fire from heaven

zechariah described plagues
smiting those fighting
against jerusalem
in the great tribulation
and biological and chemical warfare
at the battle of armageddon

the four horsemen
of the apocalypse
white horse—conquest, pestilence
red horse—war
black horse—famine
pale horse—death

idolatry
the sword
plague
wild beasts
earthquakes

break the seventh seal
the seventh trumpet is sounding

We are GOD's temples
REAL living temples
filled with GOD's glory
and housing THE HOLY SPIRIT!!!

the new world order needs a camera
or your smart phone

or a spy
to see you and keep their eye on you
to attempt to control you
but their all seeing eye is not all seeing
only YHWH
Father GOD is omnipresent,
all seeing and all knowing!!!

white throne judgment
satan and his demons
and his people
will be cast into the eternal lake of fire

believers will be caught up in the air
with JESUS

sons of jubal singing,
"where are you going to run
in a world without a border?"
fight the spirit of the anti-christ
that wants to enslave you
with a new world order!!!

soldier of light
put on your spiritual armor of GOD
it's time for fasting
and for prayer
for spiritual warfare

the mission
for our generation

if you want Lord JESUS to come back soon
heed his last request
obey the great commission
to preach HIS gospel
to every nation

i profess the name of JESUS
like a wedding vow
and after the battle of armageddon
every knee will bow
and every tongue confess
that Jesus Christ is Lord!!!!!!!

we are the church

the gathering
Jesus said, "whenever two
or more
are gathered in my name
I
I am among you"

we are the church
the church is a living Spirit
not a building or an organization
it's a local congregation
it's genuine prayer not vain repetition
it's a personal relationship with Jesus Christ
not celebrating dead tradition
it's serving the living God
not empty religion

we are the church
we are the church now
we are the church
we are the church now

in Jesus's name we claim the new birth
in Jesus's name we can cast lucifer from this earth
the gates of hell will never prevail
we cannot fail
we are the church!

we are the church
we are the church now
you are the church
you are the church now

lucifer
and every demonic principality
was defeated for all eternity
when Jesus arose from the dead
in victory
Jesus is the Spirit
but we are the body
you and me
we are the church!

we are the church
we are the church now
you are the church
you are the church now
we are the church!

i arise

you murdered me
i am a corpse in so many people's minds
with each of your words
actions
& lies
another perception of me dies
but i arise
i arise from the ashes
i arise up from the bottom
i arise, i arise!

i arise
every single morning
& get up out of bed
to meet a day filled with abuse
& injustices
& made to wear this cloak of scorn
made to apologize for my very existence
& wonder why i was even ever born
i arise!

i arise at the corners of my mouth
when i smile at you
& wish you well
as you sell
me
& everything i am
out
for the love of money
for the love of money!

i arise as i force another laugh
at the biggest joke in this town
that isn't even funny
i arise up from my knees
after praying for you
forgiving you
i arise, i arise!

i arise!
when i reach out for her hand
to walk beside me
i arise!
when i care for the elderly
i arise!
every time i hold a child
& protect it in my arms
i arise!
when danger is near
& i sound the alarm
i arise!
when i look after a younger woman
& treat her as my sister
i arise!
when i give respect to my father & mother
i arise!
every time i'm brave enough to show a stranger
who i really am
i arise, i arise!

i arise!
every time i give this benediction
& raise my voice to Heaven
it heals me
& i overcome this awful situation
& receive vindication!

Dedicated to Maya Angelou and Billy Capozzi

naked soul

my heart and soul desperately
yearns to be with you—

when will i be in your lovely presence again, my love?
how long must i wait
to gaze deeply into your eyes,
to listen to and absorb your kind, spirit filled words,
to study and memorize every inch of you?

my naked soul aches to be united with you
to once again be home
within you
and within my own skin

sukkot/blood moon—year of jubilee

sunday night september 27–monday morning september 28, 2015

four blood moons on jewish high holy days. i see the glory
of GOD in my lover's eyes. salvation. redemption. divine
intervention. freedom, tolerance. and liberty wrapped in
new prosperity. the holy of holies. my lover and me. blessed
intimacy. YHWH, JESUS, keri and me. in the holy of holies.
blessed intimacy. YHWH, JESUS, keri, zion and me. a new
family. holy holy holy. yom kippur. the blood of JESUS. it is fin-
sihed. four blood moons. sukkot. i look to the skies. it is now
jubilee! debt free prosperity. breaking the chains of slavery.
poverty. entering the promised land. liberty. no weapon can
be formed against me. i sing jubilee. worshop GOD with the
melody in my poetry. blow the shofar. how long Lord? truth
comes like a roaring lion. YHWH. GOD's DNA. within us. within
Lord JESUS. my lover keri, my son zion and me. in the holy of
holies. blessed intimacy. a new family. four blood moons. the
seven places JESUS shed his blood for us. spiritually. physically.
mentally. emotionally. socially. politically. and in this year of
jubillee- financially. restoration of all that has been stolen.
30 fold. 60 fold. 100 fold. with the blessing of new prosper-
ity. YHWH and JESUS. with THE HOLY SPIRIT bearing witness.
freedom, liberty and prosperity. joy. jubilee. i see the glory of
GOD in my lovers eyes. the year of jubilee. the year of jubilee!

circuit of silence

if life is energy. what is reality. a dream? a microchip is
like an atom. if the mirror's reflection. is just a perception.
can it redeem? a microchip is like a human cell. still water
washing over another wrinkle in your mind. when you
learn your brain is getting smaller. your humility is so
great. this is not an altered state. this is not an altered
state. [white space] white the harmony from which all
color was created. poetry and physics interface in neon
cathedral. the cyberspiritual. electronic meditation. power
surge. fire to your chakras. blessed seclusion. friendship.
the shared search. white space. the harmony. the circuit
of silence. a single cell in the body of humanity.

for christopher "dj circuit" kelly

THE GALLERY OF LIGHT: A Word of Explanation

I recite my 40-minute performance poem the gallery of light *from time to time in art galleries, cafés, and at other events with my friend DJ Circuit (Christopher Kelly) weaving a soundscape of electronic, ambient, and world music. The piece made its live debut in August 1997 at the Sage Café in Blue Point, Long Island, followed by performances at CBGB's 313 in New York (November 1998) and other venues through February 2000 and on into the 21st century.*

The gallery of light *(which I think of as "The World's First Spoken Word Rock Opera") grew out of my first widely distributed book of poetry, bearing the same title, published in 1994.*

The gallery of light *examines a character's evolution under seven different kinds of light:*

neon light (prologue)

strobe light

spotlight

moonlight

candlelight

sunlight

ultraviolet light (epilogue)

I light a candle as I welcome the audience through a new doorway into each section of this performance poem. The visual textures, comprised of video effects, photographic images, and some performance props, change with each part of the piece.

Classic rock operas such as The Who's Quadrophenia *and* Tommy, *Pink Floyd's* The Wall, *and concept albums like Nine Inch Nails'*

Downward Spiral, *all share one common thread: they depict a character's decline, driven by the evils of this world, wrongs done by parents, lovers, teachers, preachers, and supposed role models.*

In contrast, the gallery of light *features the rise of a character who starts out emotionally, spiritually, and intellectually paralyzed, then struggles toward freedom and health, step by step, as the story progresses.*

In the gallery of light *performances, I become the poem. I lie in a fetal position portraying the character who screams "my bedroom a jail cell" at the opening of the* strobe light *section. The same character reappears in the* sunlight *section, in the same position, but now as a symbol of new birth as I recite "a spiritual fetus spins in a whirlpool of color." Over the course of the poem, I become enlightened, learning that I am "a poet that is a poem, a creation that can create," and that my life, all of our lives, are a message!!! I become the poem as I turn in revelation of imagination, wisdom, and love in the a* string of pearls *performance poem.*

May your very life be a great poem!!!

I once tried to imagine what the mystical English poet William Blake might visualize and create were he alive late in the 20th century. As a result, I began writing and developing the gallery of light *as my prayer for America and the world in the 21st century.*

The gallery of light *takes after the Doors'* American Prayer *or* Supper's Ready *by Genesis. My chosen medium was electronic music, which I viewed as a new palette and canvas, which I began exploring as electronic keyboards and samplers were invented. As early industrial music developed, my experimentation evolved into a search for sounds not typically heard from keyboards, in much the same way Jimi Hendrix experimented with the electric guitar.*

My keyboard/sound module experiments with the combination of industrial music and poetry exploded with inspiration in 1989 after my alternative rock band Walk On Water changed members and became something new. I began collaborating with guitarist/ songwriter Bill Poulos, who hosted an industrial music show on Stony Brook University's WUSB. The collaboration between Bill Poulos and I helped inspire other forward-thinking musicians too, including recording artist Klayton, later of Circle Of Dust and Celldweller. In 1991, Klayton collaborated with Poulos and I to record The Poet's Eye *among his first industrial/ electronic music pieces. A few years later, these experiences informed the creation of my own* the gallery of light.

The gallery of light *live performances were realized with the influence of, and in collaboration with, artist/DJ/graphic designer Christopher "DJ Circuit" Kelly, growing organically from our close friendship.*

I believe that living with love, that loving and respecting God and all life, can overcome the all too common forces of entropy that try to perpetuate a universal downward spiral. This belief is the spirit and the womb of which this poem is born.

The gallery of light *became The Other Perspective Media's first CD release in 2006, inspiring well-known artists as well as underground creators in the years that followed. It is my hope that my work will inspire you too.*

Love and life to you! Live the other perspective!

...and welcome to the Gallery of Light!

[poet billy lamont]

for america into the 21st century

neon light

your lies are like a mist
i can't see through
my tears are a waterfall
in this river of blood
i am transparent
my heart is made of glass
the truth is fireworks
going off in the sky
and the guiding lighthouse is
the poet's eye

the truth is fireworks going off in the sky
and the guiding lighthouse is the poet's eye

my memories
are like mannequins
in a **wax museum**
standing frozen
only to become animated
when i wander
through the corridors
of my mind

my memories are like mannequins
in a wax museum
standing frozen
only to become animated
when i wander through the corridors of my mind

my
my memories are like
mannequins
in a wax museum
standing frozen
only to become animated
when i wander through the corridors
of my mind!

welcome to **the gallery of light**...

strobe light

an adult lies in the fetal position
in a strobe light generation

addicted to dreams of—
　midnight impulses
　& sugar passions

screaming,
　"my bedroom a jail cell!
　my bedroom/a jail cell"

a baby left in city traffic
getting fitted for a mental straitjacket
a sunflower with a snake at its root
a cherry tree that needs to bear fruit
metaphysical visions of a paraplegic soul

metaphysical
　　　　　visions
　　　　　　　　of a paraplegic
　　　　　　　　　　　　soul

spotlight

i
love
you
i
i...love you
ilove you/ ilove you/iloveyou/iloveyou/iloveyou

i love you
          from the bottom of my
                         current frame of reference

of course in a few years
                    i could have
                              a new preference

                 microwave romance

beware: of those who watch the parade of souls
      with microscope eyes of judgment

peripheral view
we are slaves of passion
tied to one another by habit

beware of those who watch the parade of souls with
microscope eyes of
judgment

peripheral view
we are slaves of passion tied to one another by habit

& friends are people with the same hang-ups
friends are people with the same hang-ups

& poetry is therapy?

friends/hang-ups
friends, hang-ups
poetry, therapy
poetry is therapy?

poetry is therapy!

pearls are words
words are art
art is imagination
imagination is creation
creation is life
life is experience
experience is wisdom
wisdom is love
love is **a string of pearls**

moonlight

love makes it safe to give in to desire
but should romance be a guiltless fire?
burning down my home
while forever was a nontransparent speech
to a heart as unripe as a **winter peach**

love makes it safe
to give in to desire
but should romance
be a guiltless fire?
burning down my home
while forever
was a nontransparent speech
to a heart as unripe
as a winter peach

it's all a game of chess!

it's all a game
of chess!

holding me in check
what are you trying to prove
no one watching my back
waiting for your next move

men are your court jesters
& your lover is a pawn
but the truth is my music
& minstrels sing my song

playing a game of chess with love
the cherubim never wanted to play
playing a game of chess with love
merlin sculpts you a face of clay
playing a game of chess with love
the reaper will not get his pay!

so now i'm **stranded at sea**

the waves are pounding my lifeboat
i'm struggling just to stayafloat
my sanity is drifting
as the tide is shifting

i guess i'll always be stranded at sea
outside of society it gets so lonely...
lonely
it gets so lonely

darkness surrounds me
the wind howls like a ghost
and ashes on the water
ashes on the water

now stranded in a sea so vast
i am an outcast
i am an outcast
i am an outcast!

i guess i'll always be...
stranded at sea

like **a dagger** in my heart
buried to the hilt
there's nothing more painful
than guilt

television red paint slowly drips down the pale
expressionless mannequin face

* * *

we are all parhelia.   bright colored spots of light
on a solar halo

* * *

the scapegoat of your misery is baptized with tears.
salt & light

* * *

sweating blood in the name of love in the endless
black tunnel we call **night**

candlelight

is this ministry of information
just a relic in my memory?
or a work of priceless art
on display
in the museum of my heart?
the politics of being me

my message and its reception
is based upon your experience and perception
everyone lives within their own reality
not everyone finds their spirituality
i'm climbing the stairs of loyalty
the politics of being me

is it a visual image?
or is it a mirage?
you're a master of illusion
hiding behind your facade

is it a visual image?
or is it a mirage?
and can you see beyond
your little pink corsage

insecurity!
your eyes are looking through me
insecurity!
if you only knew me
insecurity!
your eyes are looking through me
insecurity!
i am a mystery!

my heart is as deep as the deep blue sea
but can you see what's inside of me?

you lie here and bask
but i can't love a mask
you hide under covers
i can't do with temporary lovers

is it a visual image?
or is it a mirage?
either way i won't bow down
to any of your false gods!

insecurity!
your eyes are looking through me
if you only knew me
i am a mystery!

hear the call!
echoing in this hall
hear the call!
echoing in us all

what's...inside of me?
what's inside of me?
insecurity...insecurity
Lord...deliver me
Lord...
deliver me
i want to reveal
not conceal
the love that's inside of me
Lord Jesus Christ, deliver me!

the blueprint of the Spirit

the passionate
decode my message:

patience
stillness
rest
meditation
balance
endurance
laughter

i'm speaking in tongues
a riddle
decode my message:

a whisper
in the Spirit
is the blueprint of life

when a revelation from the Spirit
ignites a fire in your heart
which illuminates a vision
-sheds light on darkness-
only then gray turns to
black   and   white
a contrast
so distinct
silhouettes appear

looking through the glass veil
into the garden of paradise
the burning fire in my heart
melts my facade like ice

private vision of Jesus

red pool of passion
flooding rain of pain
infinite eyes of compassion
i'll never be the same

i'll never be the same!

sunlight

well, it's a **van gogh morning** on this gumby earth
& you with your mother teresa heart
& your cat in the hat smile should know

~the meaning of life lies within you~
dr albert schweitzer & a kazoo

a spiritual fetus
spins in a whirlpool of color
a myriad of revelations

open eyes/ open eyes/ open eyes

a baby's first breath
an old man's death
circle of ashes
circle of dust

how can a man be born when he is old?
when he is born of fire
how can a man be born when he is old?
when he is born of water
how can a man be born when he is old?
when he is born of the Spirit

a hymn in the wind
angelic choir
thoughts meant to inspire
holy fire

you want to know what makes it all worthwhile
the secrets in a child's smile
life itself is a gift

life itself is a gift!

so america...

america
this is **no kurt cobain suicide**
because sometimes i feel as if your soul
has already died

soul metamorphosis
crucifixion
& resurrection
a poet that is a poem
a creation that can create
the subconscious
sunlight
love conquers hate
LOVE conquers hate!

life as an experiment

innocence/experience

do not fear superstitions—
run without inhibitions

| walking | there are two angels | standing |
| barefoot | to every one demon* | naked |

free	the ravens fly from the tower	light
to		attracts
dance		light

smile butterfly!

white	the pupil of the eye constricts	the
rose		snake
on		is
fire		dead

no vertigo

According to the Bible, only one-third of the angels fell from glory with Satan and became demons.

sin is slavery
& sin
is a burden

                        & spirituality
                        is freedom

      satan
      you won't trap me
      in your dungeon of sin

                        the
                        snake
                        is
                        dead!

                        the
                        snake
                        is
                        dead!

      & i'm standing
      on his head

                        the
                        snake
                        is
                        dead!

      no vertigo!
      no vertigo!
      no vertigo!

dance to the rhythm of thought

    color clouds
        you were loved before you were born

    flower faces
        your soul is one of a kind

    angel kisses
        your life is precious

    love bath
        learn to love yourself
        & then you will be able to love others

see with the eyes of angels!

Dedicated to the late Allen Ginsberg

ultraviolet light

mirror eyes
you radiate watercolors
the softness of your gaze
is the art in love

& the hour
is a wildflower
untouched by the razor wind

a seed
a new birth
an open door
the quiet voice of beauty
is not something to ignore

a passionate moment of intuition
whispers your name
in silence

mirror eyes
you're my soulmate

i paint your portrait in my mind
& hang it in the gallery of light

    neon light

    strobe light

    spot light

    moonlight

    candlelight

    sunlight

    ultraviolet light

our abstract emotions
& impressionistic thoughts
awaken surreal love
as we meditate on the wisdom of
the ancient
& the young
as they intertwine
& coalesce into one
within the hand of God
in the ultraviolet light
of postmodern dreams

as we meditate on the wisdom of
the ancient
& the young
as they intertwine
& coalesce into one
within the hand of God
in the ultraviolet light
of post modern dreams

~in the ultraviolet light of post modern dreams~

are you my witness?

Jesus turning over tables in the temple
the house of worship
is not a place of business
& are you my witness?

pharisee
don't you burden me
with a weight too heavy
to carry

saducee
you love the best seat
at the party
so all can see
you make long prayers
designed to impress
but are you my witness?

i am not mocking The Holy Spirit
false prophecy comes from false prophets
but i know the truth when i hear it
& when someone is just picking my pockets

the deception
& the hate
that formed the unholy cult
heaven's gate
led the weak to an abyss
Jesus says, are you my witness?

in the name of the Father
they claim they are blessed
but on their faces you can see they are vexed
demons twist my words out of context
they seduce you with a smile
but in their hearts they hiss
are you my witness?

here's the truth of faith
& not just the myths
you will know my people by their fruit
& not their gifts
Jesus says, will you be my witness?

the fruit of the Spirit is:
love, joy, peace
long suffering
& gentleness
will you be my witness?

when money, pride
& vanity
come to steal you from our midst
you can overcome by my word
& your testimony
just greet me with charity's kiss
will you be my witness?

avoid: adultery, idolatry
witchcraft, envy, murder
& drunkenness
& such like this
will you be my witness?

when you think you are alone in isolation
eyes are really on you
& when there is heavy temptation
will you resist?
are you my witness?
Jesus says, will you be my witness?

This poem was inspired by listening to Bob Dylan songs and reading THE HOLY BIBLE.

203

words ripped from a soul still bleeding

the art
of LoVE

Real LoVE with an Inclusive Invitation
for All People, Locally
because I love locally, King
nationally because
I LoVE Americal,
and Internationally because
I LoVE ALL PEOPLE
of the world !!! :)

the invitation

Jesus says,
"will you accept true love?
my gift
grace
the remission
of the sickness
of sin

the invitation
redemption
by my blood
a sacred threshold
through love's sanctification

speak to me with your prayers
be my friend
in me there is no end
eternity
infinity

in Jah, Jehovah God
in me
with The Holy Spirit
The Holy Trinity
infinity

will you accept true love?
my gift
grace
forgiveness
eternal life
sealed with a holy kiss

I love you
will you be my witness?"

take a moment to reflect, meditate, and pray

Beyond the Stars

My world was in black and white
Nothing inside of me
You painted my world with colors
Making me see, see in 3-D

Your home is beyond the stars
Your home is beyond the stars in paradise
Your love fills the universe
Like lightning lights the sky
Your words fill my heart
Like thunder from on high

My world was in darkness
A blind man in the night
The photograph came into focus
You turned on the light!

Your home is beyond the stars
Your home is beyond the stars in paradise
Your love fills the universe
Like lightning lights the sky
Your words fill my heart
Like thunder from on high

Your home is beyond the stars
Your home is beyond the stars
in paradise

a song of praises

I was swimming in a sea of doubt
Drowning in a pool of pride
Caught in a wave of pain
Going with the tide

I was standing in the storm of life
Blowing in a hurricane
Saved in a wind of change
You are the shelter from the rain

I sing the song of ages
That a band of angels sing
I sing a song of praises
To Jesus Christ the king

I'm crossing the fields of slavery
Entering the promised land
Ringing the bells of liberty
The faith to take your hand

I sing the song of ages
That a band of angels sing
I sing a song of praises
To Jesus Christ the king
...to Jesus Christ the king!

The Book of Life has many pages
oh, Lord, make my life a song of praises!

Jah beautiful

albert einstein
is the universe a friendly place?
every moment precious few
i want to paint your pretty face
all the colors will be hopeful
reflections of Jah beautiful

greetings new breed
we are made for eternity
not for time
imagine a dream with originality
not with mime
you have your own fingerprints

fascination
admiration
experience God
a starry night
the coral sea
Jesus, you have revealed yourself to me
blessed intimacy
sacred, holy
sacred, holy
you are light
science is beginning to see
your interdimensional reality
holy, holy, holy
pure clear genuine true
all within us cries out for life!
all praises joyful!
reflections of Jah beautiful

today i remembered me

today i remembered me—
renewed my mind
shed a skin
of past trauma
of mental slavery

today i remembered me—
blew off the dust from the pages
of my writing and books
and was set free
when i declared liberty
and freedom
from the jail of society
today, i remembered me

today i remembered me—
the meaning of life within me
i recognized THE HOLY SPIRIT
the GOD in me
today i remembered to make sure i had a good night's sleep
to eat right, healthy
to follow and respect THE SPIRIT that upholds life
and got reacquainted with the artist i was born to be
today i remembered not pride, but dignity
today, i remembered me

today i remembered me—
to guard my heart
but to be open to love
with a boundary that is healthy

i remembered to be the ART
to be the PEACE, to be the LOVE
today, i remembered me

today i remembered me—
a poet, an artist, a writer,
not just a worker bee
not just a cog in your wheel
another interchangeable body
not just a father
a son, a brother
a fiance, a lover
a consumer, a credit score
today i remembered me

yesterday i was kicked off the ladder of success
the american dream is a lie!
the american dream sure was a great idea
the american dream we cannot let it die!

society keeps telling me,
"you cannot write today
you have too many responsibilities"—
but when i do write
i will be ferocious!
when i write
the page will bleed with light!
when i write
when i write!
today i remembered me

a blank pure white page for you,
the reader, to write your life.
your goals. your inspirations.

Imagine a Day!
Your Life Is a Message!

[billy lamont]

Poems for the Future
august 29, 2019, new york city

identity

we are born looking for identity
needing a home, security
intuitively looking for
the LOVE of a family
& to be a part of a healthy community
so we can grow into our destiny
& leave a legacy
an inheritance for the next generation—
the blessing of a better life
not a burden
for our children

imagination

imagination, with wisdom
as well as knowledge,
to pioneer and innovate
this is the distance and difference
between doing something merely good
and being Great!!!

a few breaths

breathe in
breathe out
in
out
breathe in mercy
let go of worry
breathe in grace
breathe out compassion
breathe in forgiveness
let go of bitterness
breathe in faith
faith
let go of fear
a few breaths
in
out
in
out
let it go!

two swans

oxygen kisses
[love is a gas mask in the poison smog]

lying with her on the bed
closely, but never touching
we are facing each other in the fetal position
the outline of our forms
make a heart
like two angel white swans making love
symbiotic pure love

under a mystical shavuot ny city pentecost sunset

Looking at the Brooklyn Bridge on a Summer Night

barefoot in walt whitman's leaves of grass
feeling the calling of *Poets To Come*
breathing in—contemplating America
breathing out—meditating The World
I'm vibrating with the call to follow JESUS
to Love GOD is to Love People
from my soul to the world
in the east river of our collective consciousness
soul magnet, shiny beads of color in the night sky
at the end of the world

or is this the sky of new beginnings?
hope paints watercolors in the rapturous brooklyn sky
swirling circles of color
   beads of light—yellow, blue, red, purple
   out of focus,
   like christmas tree lights decorating new york city skyscrapers
   white circles, like a string of pearls hanging from the neck
   of a metallic kingdom gateway
   spots of color like arthur rimbaud's color of vowels
   like color sound echoing in the dark water's mystery

   yellow jasper beads of light
   fire from the sun

	temperatures
are rising!	natural disasters
are increasing!	northern glaciers
are melting!	devastating
low sea level areas	leaving
refugees fleeing!	nuclear tensions

between countries are reaching boiling!
the emergency of global warming!!!
is anyone listening?
global corporation money is co-opting
elections, what should be We The People governments
as we feast on poison food
ingest toxic water
as our people, animals, fish, birds, trees, plants, insects
are diseased and dying!
our newborn babies lay crying,
"What is our future?!!"

hungry, for real organic food
thirsty, in need of clean drinking water
for all!!!

fire from Heaven
the heart chakra radiates all the colors of the rainbow
my heart is ripe with words
seeds of hope, love and life
my heart has lips
"Create don't destroy."

blue beads of light
a new blue sings the blues -
for all the enslaved woman
for all the oppressed
and suppressed
i too am singing the blues
a miles davis *Kind of Blue* jazz blues
for women, for every victim

including our children
murdered by gun violence
sold into slavery
a new blue sings the blues
for all to live with freedom and in liberty
a new blue sings the blues
and i too sing the blues
for everyone to fulfill their potential
and destiny
without any limits
all inclusively
oh may all woman, children, men, the outcasted victims
be able to live with holy dignity!!!
and sensitivity

~ sensitivity ~
the fragrance of light
the color of sound
the texture of breath
the flavor of fire
the tonality of love

blood red beads of light
                splatters the night sky
like paint on a canvas
                from jackson pollock's paintbrush
red beads of light
                for the blood spilled
of the native american
                for the slavery
of the african
                all covered with the redeeming

healing blood of JESUS
          We are grafted in
grafted into
          GOD's vine
into GOD's bloodline
          all inclusively!!!
no need to overcomplicate fate
we just need to simply believe and receive
the blessing of unconditional LOVE from
~ the sacred heart of JESUS ~
          the seven places JESUS shed His blood
          bloody heart tears of LOVE for You and I
          for our eternal victory!!!
          spiritually
          mentally
          physically
          emotionally
          socially
          politically
          and financially!!!
          for everyone's prosperity
          and their family!
          blessed all inclusively!
          blessed
          We The People, Citizens Of The World
          locally
          nationally
          internationally

to be whole
we need whole-i-ness
holiness

everything our hands touch is blessed!
every place our feet walk is blessed!

    - incense breath of prayer
    fills the air -
    Faith With Action Is Alive!!!

purple beads of light
the royal priesthood of the everyday believer!
compassion passion empathy
in one person is a universe!
a verse
one new man
oh Lord, renew my mind
and paint it purple
purple, purple
purple brain!

visions on the inside of closed eyelids
outsiders and insiders
we know the answers to every question
know LOVE
know PEACE
know intuitive pure

    the heart
    the mind
    the body
    the soul
    the breath
    the soul lives in our gut
    - our intuition -

we are living temples of GOD!
YHWH breathed life into us
on the day of creation
meditate the WORD of GOD
until your heart and mind
BELIEVE it and Feel it
in your INTUITION
- the eyes of THE SPIRIT -

meditation vision
not without mind
but with PEACE
in a quiet mind

meditate the WORD of GOD
until your heart and mind
BELIEVE it and Feel it
in your INTUITION
with new vision
with new eyes
         exhale,
breathe life into the world
new life
now verbalize it
hear yourself say it
LOVE
PEACE
now You and I
can be the WORD
be the POEM
pure soul think

oh new york city where so many of my new dreams are born
all beads of color dissolve
into streaming white opals of light
laying in walt whitman's leaves of grass
Looking At The Brooklyn Bridge On A Summer Night

the frequency of life: love vibrations

floating, floating, floating
on your mind's wave
the frequency of life
vibrates with creation

we are energy
made up of cells
electrons, the smallest part of a cell
is energy, vibrating -
that energy is sound
our own, unique, magnificent song!!!

the music within me
the fabric of life
YHWH's frequency
- our soul song -
  soulful—>wonderful
  dancing in our cells
- love vibrations -

the micro, the macro lens
even my cells sing praises to YHWH!!!!!!!!!
the tree within
the Creator in me
YHWH—>sighs—>
the breath of life
- love vibrations -
of The Spirit
the idea has life
is alive, is alive, IS ALIVE!!!
the idea, the idea
the words

blossom, create
vibrate, vibrate
forms ourselves
reforms our world!
- the frequency of light -

ABOUT THE AUTHOR

Billy Lamont is an American poet with an avant-garde approach to writing, music, performance art, politics, and film. At the heart of his poetry is the passion to inspire hope and to be a voice for everyday people. His unique vision for poetry into the 21st century, combined with a belief in the power of words for creation, reformation, and healing brought his influence from grassroots to national success in the 1990s and then international recognition in the new millennium. His work encourages dignity, upholds life, and serves as a catalyst for a world of readers and listeners, both in the mainstream and on society's fringes. He inspires many to live in a more loving way and to feel for different justice causes for the first time, to help with personal and social reform in this Global Age.

Poet Billy Lamont has performed on MTV and Much Music Television and appeared on radio stations across the United States. Lamont has also performed at many rock festivals, including touring with Lollapalooza '94, '95, 2003 and Cornerstone Festival 2004 and 2006. Due to the success of his first book of poems *The Gallery of Light*, distributed by Ingram, Lamont has given book signings at book stores such as Barnes and Noble in shopping malls across the United States. The follow up, *strobe light generation* fueled Lamont's passionate and thought-provoking multimedia shows that combine his performance poetry with electronic music and synchronized film. His latest poetry with electronic/Americana pop music CD/digital download is entitled *Beyond Babylon*.

Lamont's third major volume of poetry *Words Ripped from a Soul Still Bleeding* is a powerful successor to his earlier books and audio releases like *billy lamont with the peculiar people* and *Beyond Babylon*. Lamont's entire CD/digital download catalog is distributed by The Orchard internationally.

His 1998 debut CD *Into the 21st Century* was a benefit for Teen Challenge, with performances by two of his greatest influences, the legendary Allen Ginsberg and the incredible Mike Peters of The Alarm on the title track. In his later years, Ginsberg expressed love and support for Lamont's poetry with permission to use an audio sample from his first recital of the Beat Generation epic poem *Howl*.

In 2014, Lamont collaborated with Mike Peters again, as well as many other rock stars and inclusive of everyday artists, on the recording *The Scriptures* to help foster peace between Muslims, Christians, and Jews in The Holy Land. *The Scriptures* is a benefit for Love Hope Strength Foundation and those fighting cancer. Lamont's contribution to *The Scriptures* earned him a Guinness World Record as part of "The World's Longest Officially Released Song."

Lamont's career was also promoted by Larry Norman, widely known as the Father of Christian Rock. The music legend invited Lamont to open several of his shows from 1998–2000 and to become an artist on Norman's own Solid Rock Records The result was an album of compositions written for release on Solid Rock, with preliminary sessions produced by Norman in 2000. However, Norman's failing health made further sessions impossible. The album was never completed, and the session tapes went missing from Norman's archives. Lamont returned the favor of support by raising awareness and funding for Norman's emergency healthcare with the CD/ download *billy lamont with the peculiar people.*

During the creation of Lamont's *strobe light generation* book of poetry, he was also being encouraged by legendary poet/ peace activist, Jesuit priest, the late Daniel Berrigan, as well as being kindly affirmed by the brilliant Peter Garrett, the front man of Midnight Oil and the former Australian Federal Minister of Environmental Protection, Heritage, Arts and Education.

All these experiences and influences are a huge part of Lamont's vision for the future! In his recent poetry, he encourages brothers and sisters globally to "Imagine A Day, we need an intelligent heart, a loving mind, LOVE, intelligence of the heart will light your mind!"

Lamont's three major book releases and eight CDs/digital downloads are available through most major distributors such as amazon.com, barnesandnoble.com, and iTunes.com and can be streamed and listened to on spotify.com, iTunes.apple.com, googleplay.com, YouTube.com, tidal.com, and many other popular sites.

Poet Billy Lamont, c/o The Other Perspective Media. 631-981-4780, TOPm777@gmail.com, billylamont.com
Facebook: facebook.com/poet.lamont; Twitter: twitter.com/poetbillylamont; Instagram: instagram.com/poetbillylamont; YouTube: sage777billy

More available at BillyLamont.com:

The Gallery Of Light –
1994 book of poems, $10.00

strobe light generation –
2005 book of poems, $19.95

into the 21st century –
1998 poetry with music CD/digital download, $10.00

billy lamont with the peculiar people –
2004 handmade poetry chapbook with music CD, $7.00 (SOLD OUT),
available as digital download

painkiller –
2006 poetry with music CD/digital download, $10.00

hedge of thorns –
2008 poetry with music CD, $7.00 (SOLD OUT)

the gallery of light –
2009 poetry with music CD, (not for sale, only available as a gift)

renegade of hope –
2009 spoken word CD//digital download, $7.00

outlaw of love –
2010 spoken word CD/digital download, $7.00

billy lamont with the peculiar people –
May 2011 professional quality CD re-release of 2004 poetry with
music CD, $7.00

Beyond Babylon –
2013 poetry with music CD/digital download, $10.00

Hedge Of Thorns –
2015 Will You Be My Witness? Four Blood Moons limited edition
re-release of 2008 poetry with music CD, $7.00

Words Ripped From A Soul Still Bleeding –
2017 book of poems, $14.95

Words Ripped From A Soul Still Bleeding, Poems For The Future Edition –
2019 book of poems, $10

Inside Book Blurbs:

Mike Peters

"There's no truth like the truth you dare to let yourself see. Billy's poetry lets you see the truth of himself, and the truth that surrounds him, which is also the truth that surrounds you. Take a look and you will find love, hate, all life in it."

Mike Peters is a Welsh singer/songwriter for the rock band The Alarm. He is co-founder of Love Hope Strength Foundation, whose purpose is to raise funds and awareness in order to benefit people with cancer and leukemia. He received The Most Excellent Order of the British Empire rewarding his chivalry, contributions to the arts, and work with charitable organizations.

Joe Franklin

"In the tradition of Jim Morrison, Bob Dylan, Patti Smith, and Jim Carroll comes Billy Lamont...and I love it!"

The late Joe Franklin was the Host of the *Joe Franklin Show,* the longest running television talk show ever.

Dave Kendall

"Billy Lamont is in possession of a strange and compelling vision."

Dave Kendall was the host of MTV's innovative *120 Minutes* show.